I Will Meet You
On The Other Side

I WILL MEET YOU ON THE OTHER SIDE

THAMI NODWELE

PARTRIDGE

A Penguin Random House Company

Print information available on the last page.

To order additional copies of this book, contact
Toll Free 0800 990 914 (South Africa)
+44 20 3014 3997 (outside South Africa)
orders.africa@partridgepublishing.com

www.partridgepublishing.com/africa

CONTENTS

ACKNOWLEDGEMENT

I never thought of writing any book in my life of any kind. To me that was too much work and I did not have extra time of sitting and writing. Though, sometimes it crossed my mind like anybody who would have thoughts of writing but not being serious about it.

I thank my tutor at seminary Mr. Hank Pott (USA) who saw a potential in me and highly encouraged me to do so. He went as far as giving me a time frame when to finish. Like he knew if he did not do that I might have relaxed and thought that I will do it someday but end up not doing it.

There were also many other tutors at the seminary who also played a big role in shaping my life academically and spiritually. I am also thankful of those tutors as I have learned a lot from them.

When I was doing one of Mr. Pott's subjects I had this feeling that he might be a very strict person and that if I do not put all my efforts I might not do well in his subject. I had therefore worked hard to get good grades in his subject. I sincerely thank the Lord for him.

Mr. Pott was like he got a direct instructions from the Lord what he was supposed to tell me because except about writing. He gave me advises about my relationship with God and things I needed to do to grow spiritually and he was always specific.

INTRODUCTION

Frank grew up without his biological parents. He was raised by his grandmother after he was abandoned by his mother. He grew up in a dysfunctional environment. This prompted him to learn fighting at an early age for self-defense and the protection of his siblings. His little brother was brutally murdered by thugs at an early age while they were still growing and having dreams of becoming something in life.

His youngest sister disappeared without trace. Every effort was made to trace her for years but without any success. All these things happened after his little brother for some time had been predicting his death and the disappearance of their younger sister without trace.

The younger brother used to tell the family that the time would come that he would leave this world because he did not belong to this earth. He used to tell them that he was a visitor on this earth.

This devastated Frank badly as part of him was taken away from him. A person he loved so much and regarded as the only little brother he had and knew whom he was raised with. That had a very negative impact in him as he started to lose interest in life and did not care much what could happen to him.

It took him a long time to accept the death of his little brother that he could continue again to face life. He eventually realized that life needed to go on without his brother and nothing he could do to bring him back. He had always hoped that his little sister would be found some day.

From tough life he experienced at an early age he was determined to defend himself in all situations even in the most dangerous circumstances. He never compromised his beliefs even when he started working. He refused to be used as an instrument to destroy others' careers. He would ask for clarification for any suspicious task and if no proper explanation given he would reject it.

He played a big role in helping the poor and the dispossessed during the apartheid government. He was known of defending the families who were faced with eviction from their homes. In every situation he was involved he managed to help many people who were unfairly treated and despised.

He challenged bad leadership in society and in corporate environment. He rejected the idolization of the rich and famous. Instead he embraced the poor and recognized them as human beings and supported them.

He encouraged the grooming and training of leaders for the future when the present leaders would not be there. He was greatly frustrated by the leaders who failed to give direction and lead their communities.

Frank stood strongly against the attacking of foreign nationals and their churches. He believed if people could decide to accuse others with serious accusations. They should first do serious investigation before they could come to a conclusion of some sort.

He never gave up fighting against the injustices irrespective of the consequences he might face. He paid a big price for not wanting to collaborate with the oppressors and the corrupt system.

Frank had a vision of the spiritual beings in the spiritual world. He also had a vision of the recession which affected the whole world and his country before it took place. He disagreed with many religious practices which were practiced by his community which was not scriptural.

He was not afraid to express his views about anything which was not proper and did not do things to please the others.

CHAPTER 1

Frank was born six months pre-matured. After six months he was rejecting the breast fed milk and for some reason he was abandoned to his grandmother to raise him in the outskirts of a small town called Dundee. According to his grandmother he was very sick as a child and she did not think he was going to make it but he survived.

Frank grew up under difficult and of poor conditions but his grandmother took care of him under all those conditions and treated him like her own child. During his upbringing around the age of three or maybe even before that he was able to see spiritual beings which no other normal human being could be able to see with the naked eye. It emerged one night while he was sleeping with his grandmother, at midnight he was awake and to his astonishment there was a man inside the room staring at him and what was unusual the door was locked which could have allowed any intruder to access the house.

By the look of it this man was not going to hurt him as a child the way it appeared and he was not scared that he was awake and that he could scream. Frank covered his head and hide towards his grandmother and he never told anyone about this incident. It also occurred when there was a ritual ceremony at one of his relatives' house that he was able to see some strange creatures in human form moving around from the gate and all around where the celebration was taking place. No one else could see these creatures except him because everyone was jolly not saying anything about some uninvited guests.

It was a bit uncomfortable for him, having some fear because those creatures were not nice looking and he was also scared that they might harm him. He was not sure whether they were able to notice that he could see them or not. He could not tell either anybody about what he was seeing.

It did not end up there because at some stage they were sleeping outside the house because it was very hot in summer with his elder brother and their cousins, again around midnight there was this man who was standing on top of something under the tree looking up the sky just next to the place where they were sleeping. It never crossed his mind to report this incident as well.

To his understanding as he grows and became a Christian, he came to a conclusion that what he saw during that ceremony were demons. The only thing which still puzzled him was the human figures he saw inside the house and the one under a tree. He was still not sure whether were also these demons or angels or wizards hoping someday he will get their revelations.

Growing up without the biological parents for Frank was not easy at all. He was vulnerable to all sorts of abuse but his grandmother protected him in whatever situation where she could, which took place at her presence. His elder brother, Joshua was also raised by his grandmother and he was really like a big brother towards him.

Frank remembered very vividly that he gave his elder brother a lot of run around. One day he happened to pick up some cents on the road and he asked him to keep them for him, it was not long Frank wanted the money back to buy sweets. His elder brother tried to convince him not to but Frank was crying throwing himself on the ground and he had to give him his money back.

It could be he acted like that taking advantage because he knew it was his big brother and he was soft to him. As much as some of his relatives were abusive to Frank but they did demonstrate some love towards him at some stage.

A year before Frank was about to start school his grandmother, his cousin sister and Frank took a journey to a village where his grandmother grew up. Frank was excited about the journey. However, immediately he found himself in some strange place before they reach the destination he wanted to go back home.

He was crying and tried to walk back home he thought it was just that simple that he could walk back. What was strange his cousin sister Deliwe was younger than him and instead of being the one who throws tantrums she was calm and understanding.

However, when they finally arrived at the village he was now quiet and seemed to enjoy the place but it was not for long.

One thing he did not like about the village life, children were not treated like children. The children were also expected to work in the plantation with adults. There was also this old man who was his grandmother's brother who wanted that his grandmother must leave Frank behind when they go back home. To Frank that was a real nightmare but his grandmother refused and told him that Frank needed to go to school and his mother will never allow that Frank be uneducated.

Something terrible happened to Frank while they were still in the village which made him always feel ashamed to relate. Young as he was there was an older girl who abused him. This is one of the most gruesome acts to happen to a child whether a girl or a boy. Your innocence is compromised at an early stage of your life you will never be the same again, unless by the grace of the Lord you could be able to overcome that bad experience.

When the day arrived that they should go back home that was one of the most exciting moments of Frank's life. He still remembered that he had earrings in his ears and the first thing he requested was that they be removed from his ears as boys did not wear earrings in the township. They eventually left by bus and connected a train in some town which he did not know and it could be it took them two days to reach home.

Frank was happy to be back at home and he had two younger cousin brothers Caesar and Israel whom they left behind when they took a journey and he was so happy to see them again because he loved them very much. Unfortunately one of them Israel passed away around that time of the year and Frank was very sad. He asked his grandmother whether they will ever see him again; his grandmother told him they will not because he was gone forever. Frank thought if at least his grandmother could have said something different because it hurt him so much the fact to know that he would never ever see one his little brothers again.

It could be his grandmother was unable to explain to a child that when somebody dies they do not come back to this present life. Only those who are still alive will go to those who are gone when each of their time arrives. Until then it was not possible.

Early the following year Frank was required to start school. When the date arrives unfortunately he was not prepared for the big day therefore he was a bit resisting in going to school. He had a certain aunt who originated from Lesotho who seemed to enjoy his fear of going to school and she was patronising him about the whole issue. That made Frank to actually hate school from the very first day. He could not understand the whole purpose that why he should go to school.

As a result he had to repeat the first grade because he was not interested in this schooling business. He also viewed the teacher of his class as the ferocious person who was ever chastising children for every mistake they made.

Sometimes Frank used to hide under the benches to avoid being punished.

After his grandmother recognised that Frank hates school, she explained to him the whole purpose of going to school. That it was important that he gets educated so that he could be able to get a decent job and look after himself when he is an adult. More important for him being educated she told him that he was an orphan and he did not have anything to inherit from anybody like money which could help him to survive. Also that she was not rich that she could leave him these benefits when she dies. The only thing which she could help him with was to pay for his school fees and buy books until he finishes school.

This explanation definitely made sense to Frank because from then on he took his school work very serious and he started to do well at school and he enjoyed going to school. As he was growing he had a bad tendency of fighting with his big brother Joshua. It was not making sense what was wrong with him and his big brother was far older than him with almost ten years difference.

There was this day when his elder brother was busy with his homework for whatever reason Frank had a fight him. He took one of the books his brother was busy with and tore it into two pieces. To retaliate his brother took one of Frank's books too and only tore the cover from the whole book. Their grandmother was very upset of this fighting of Frank and his brother. She reprimanded both of them that they should refrain from ever fighting. Frank was remorseful and regretted deeply, of first disrespecting his big brother and secondly the malicious damage he did to his book and his brother's retaliation which was a minor damage than what he did to his book.

From that day Frank made a vow to himself that he would never again disrespect his big brother and fight him for whatever reason. He decided even if his brother could be on the wrong and beat him he will never fight him back again. From nowhere there was a complete change in Frank and he never fought with his big brother or demonstrates any disrespect against him. He developed a high respect of him and got along well with him. Although they never lived together after his brother left school they still phoned each other and chat like brothers.

Frank's cousin sister Deliwe was fetched by her mother before she could start school and went to Cape Town. After she left Frank realised how much he loved and missed her but something unusual happened. While Frank was still in primary school his grandmother told him that his cousin sister was going to get married. Frank protested to his grandmother that they should not allow such a thing to happen because she was still a child and she needed to get educated and finish school. Anyway she got married and unfortunately that marriage never lasted long she was divorced and without proper education.

Years after Frank left school when he was attending his grandmother's funeral after she passed on. Frank was told that his cousin sister was married for the second time and she died previous year after she was sick. Hearing this news Frank was filled with agony he was asking himself what crime could his poor cousin sister have committed to deserve the kind of cruelty she experienced. She was deprived of her childhood and now she died pre-matured and maybe it could have been because of poor lifestyle she lived which was caused by her early marriage.

CHAPTER 2

Frank encountered a lot of hardship as time goes on as life was changing towards him and not kind to him anymore. Boys were rough in the street and he had to use his fighting skills as he was trained to fight at an early age. However, fighting back was not a recommended option because at home it was forbidden. In frequent situations the boys who used to start a fight with him he would defeat them. They would in turn go and report him and get him in trouble.

When you are frequently punished you become stubborn and hostile to those around you. You distrust that person who continues punishes you and have the impression that they treat you bad because you are not their child. That was the feeling Frank had when he found himself in trouble.

Unfortunately as a child it was very easy to make mistakes than to do right and that always got him into trouble. When he was attacked and injured by a certain older boy no one could be on his side. One evening they were playing as children at the next door neighbor's yard and one older boy also from the same neighborhood came and started to push Frank towards a fence without any provocation. He pushed him until he fell on the fence with his right hand side of his body. Frank sustained a terrible injury on the side of his body something very sharp cut him and he could not establish whether it was a barbwire or what.

He felt such a severe pain from the injury and he wept because of the pains he was feeling. All the other boys came to check what was wrong and he was bleeding profusely. They helped him to get home his uncle was home with his friend and his grandmother also came out of the house to see what was happening.

When they checked where he was injured and saw the wound, his grandmother remarked that she had never seen such an acute wound in her whole life. That gave Frank an impression that he was badly injured. The boys who helped him home reported who did that to him but nothing was done about it. Instead Frank was blamed for playing in the street at night. He was taken to hospital by a relative's car.

When they arrived at the hospital there was no doctor and the nurses phoned a doctor but the doctor could not come and he instructed them what they should do. Frank could hear that they were planning to stitch the wound he cried very hard so that they do not stitch him being scared for further pains. They phoned the doctor again and explained to him that it was not going to be possible because of the way he was crying.

The doctor advised them not to stitch the wound but to clean it with an antistatic, put some medicine and bandage it because that is what they did. He was given some pills as well probably pain killers and they were told that Frank's uncle should bring him back for a checkup. Frank still has a terrible scar on his right hand of his body from that injury to this day.

After this incident Frank avoided reporting any bad experiences which happened to him because of fearing that he would be blamed. In another incident he injured himself trying to climb a tree to wrap a back yard zip liner from one branch of a tree to another. He stole this zip liner from other boys who were his relatives because they did not want to play with him. He went with his schoolmates to remove it from the trees it was wrapped. They went to wrap it away from the original place so that the owners could not find it.

While he was trying to climb on the first tree to wrap it but when he was almost at the branch he was going to wrap it on. He lost balance and he fell on the ground spraining his ankle. He could not be able to stand up and walk.

His friends had to organise a bicycle to take him home. He had to warn them beforehand that when they arrive at home they must not say he fell from a tree they must rather say he got injured while they were playing a football to avoid getting him into trouble. When they arrive at Frank's house there was nobody at home and they helped him to get off the bicycle and helped him to get inside the house.

Frank's foot started to swell and became worse around in the evening and when everybody had arrived from work. When he was asked what happened he said he fell and got injured while he was playing soccer with his schoolmates. That was an issue he was questioned why was he playing soccer. This question really sounded ridiculous because he was a child and a child's job is to play most of the time.

He could not answer that question because there was no answer for it. The following day he was now completely not able to walk he could only crawl. It took him almost three weeks to be able to walk again and all this time he could not go to school. It could be on the third week that he was able to go to school limping. His teacher did not ask him why he was not coming to school all along he guessed maybe his friends told her.

After school late in the afternoon Frank's teacher arrived at Frank's house accompanied by one of her daughters and everybody was back from work. She pleaded with Frank's family that they needed to take him to hospital because it was possible that he had broken his ankle as he was still limping after so long after the incident.

Frank's grandmother agreed that he would be taken to hospital the following day. Just after his teacher left he was yelled at that money would be wasted on him to be taken to hospital and yet it was his own fault that he got injured. Anyway the following day he was told to go to the government clinic rather and it was cheaper at the clinic. At the clinic they applied some ointment on his ankle and bandaged it and that was it.

He went to school the day after and his teacher called him she asked how was his ankle. Frank told her it was better but she was not convinced. She asked him whether he went to hospital, Frank told her that he was sent to the clinic and he was bandaged. She expressed her disappointment and pointed out. That the reason she wanted that he be taken to hospital was that the leg was going to be put on an ex-ray to ascertain whether it was not broken. However, Frank survived that and continued with his life.

His teacher tried her best to help him but she could not do more than what she did. This was the teacher who discovered that Frank had a good voice in singing. She made him to sing soprano with the girls in the choir. Frank used to stand in the front row between the girls when singing.

When the choir was singing out of tune particularly the soprano, she would tell everybody to stop singing. Then she would ask Frank to sing alone, after that she would ask the soprano whether they heard how he sang. If they replied yes she would tell them to sing and if they sang out of tune again she would take a stick and give them hiding.

She would let Frank sing again until they get the song right. During Frank's final year at that school as he was going to another primary school she was also leaving the same year. Before she left, she advised Frank that he should never damage his voice by trying to sing a bass. She told him that he had a beautiful good voice and he must not stop singing.

Unfortunately Frank did not take her advice and at the school he went. The class teacher who was also their music teacher had less interest in grooming children to sing. Although the principal of his former school also came to this same school with Frank and told his class teacher about Frank singing abilities but it made no difference. Frank also did not have much interest either in singing except singing at church and not singing soprano as he was advised.

After a couple of years Frank had parted with his music teacher he met her on school holidays in another town. Frank greeted her she responded but not looking at him, Frank thought she did not recognise him anymore. However, she turned around and looked at him and asked him whether he was still singing in a choir, Frank agreed telling lies because he did not want to disappoint her.

Inside Frank felt bad for lying and also not having kept his promise that he would keep on singing. This reminded him the story in the Bible (Matthew 25:14-24) New King James Revised a man who went travelling to a far country who called his servants and delivered his goods to them. To each according to his own ability and immediately he went on a journey. The two made profit of what they were left with.

One who received one talent decided to go and dig in the ground and hid his lord's money. Frank felt he did like this lazy wicket servant and did not pursue his singing talent although it was confirmed by a professional music teacher that he did have the talent. Frank felt guilty and repented. He asked for forgiveness to the Lord unconditionally.

After that he was able to encourage many young people not to take their talents lightly and that they should work hard in developing them. There were many who never had an opportunity to demonstrate their talents and died before they could do so. Their dreams faded away and not of because they were lazy but never had mentors who could help them to achieve their dreams.

When Frank went to secondary school he had to be forced to sing. His new friends he found at secondary school were singing and they had to report him to the music teacher that he should sing. Unfortunately Frank could not go back to his past and fix things which went wrong in his life. He must thank the Lord because where he messed up the Lord has already forgiven him.

CHAPTER 3

Still discussing about Frank's early life, there was another man who was also a relative of Frank. He used to like Frank because Frank used to stand up for himself against older boys. Sometimes they used to play next to his house and he would listen as they were arguing as boys. He would be impressed with Frank when he listens because of the way Frank used defend himself in argument against the older boys.

He really showed love to Frank which he hardly experienced at home. He would give him some of his radios which he was not using. One day he gave his son money to go with Frank to the movies. He wanted that they should watch a movie which was playing that weekend called, "King of kings." Unfortunately it was not playing and there was a cowboy movie playing instead.

Frank and his son went to watch that movie and to them it was a good movie as it was full of action and that is what they liked as children. After the movie they went home and they told him that "King of kings" did not play and they watched a different movie. They could see the disappointment in his face and he told them that movie was about Jesus Christ.

Since after that, Frank got an explanation about the movie "King of kings." Although he had never seen the movie, he loved the name "King of kings." After this old man's son matriculated Frank was told his wife and his son left him. At that time Frank was in boarding school. Frank saw the old man when he visited home on school holidays he did not look good at all. He was drowning himself into alcohol. He died after a while Frank left school. The relatives struggled to get hold of his wife and his son because the wife was destroying every correspondence she received informing them about his death.

Frank felt sad whenever he thought about this old man who cared for him and yet he never demonstrated any sympathy towards him. He could have paid him a visit in his house at his moment of despair. After his family had forsaken him at least Frank was supposed to let him know that he loved and cared for him. The only thing that Frank could hope for now was that his soul was in heaven.

However, Frank was quiet and respectful as a result his other uncle who was younger than the one who used to beat him bought him clothes, a shirt and a trouser because Frank could not curse compared to his younger cousin brother Caesar. What Frank found not fair was that the adults seemed to be entertained by the strong language his cousin used and he was not reprimanded. Therefore the little boy did not see anything wrong of what he was saying.

Although Frank was happy for the new clothes he was sad at the same time because his little cousin got nothing. He felt if his uncle could have bought him something less than completely not to buy him anything. Anyway there was nothing he could do or suggest about that he had to be grateful of what he got.

During those early years of his growing his aunt, Caesar's mother was nominated to be a Sunday school teacher and the Sunday school was held at their house. That was one thing Frank enjoyed so much he always looked forward to the Sunday so that he could go to Sunday school. He was so enthusiastic with Sunday school and would answer all the questions which were asked. It was so lovely for him more than the normal school.

It did not last long because Frank's aunt relocated to another town and the other lady who was also a Sunday school teacher passed away. The only thing which they could attend now was church. The church was boring because it did not cater for the children. Even the way they sang was so boring because most were old people who could not sing well. They were ever out of tune in whatever song they were singing.

Eventually Frank left this church leaving his little cousin Caesar behind. He went to join Anglican Church which was the original church of the family. At least he enjoyed there because there were many young people and the church was full of life.

He spent most of his time in his uncle's gymnasium after school or playing with his friends from school who were staying far from his house. His grandmother used to complain about that he played far from home. She taught he could end up hanging around with wrong boys and maybe learns committing crime and end up in jail. On Sundays he would go to church, he started to serve as an altar boy and end up in singing in the choir.

There was nothing much common with him and the boys of his street compared to his schoolmates. With his schoolmates they also attended same the church and they shared a lot in common. Caesar his little cousin complained to him that he went to join Anglican Church and left him behind because he was young and could not make decisions of his own. Frank felt bad because he was telling the truth he should have asked him to join him.

Frank loved his little brother and he did not like to see him hurting as much as his little cousin sister Nono who was a daughter of his uncle. At home Frank was regarded as the elder child therefore he was expected to clean in the house and look after his siblings when the adults were not at home as his elder brother was far older than the rest of them and was regarded as an adult. At school he did not like to be bullied so he fought anybody who would try and give him trouble. He defended is little brother too when attacked by the older boys.

One thing Frank never used to do when growing up was to start a fight; he only defended himself whenever he was being attacked. He would also defend the other boys who could not fight for themselves. There was a time when he was at secondary school just after school riots. They decided that

19

as boys they should shave their heads in mourning of those who were killed by the apartheid government.

A certain boy could not shave his head because it was against his custom to shave his head. This boy was attacked by all the other boys who were around him. They were using all sorts of instruments. Fortunately no sharp object was used until Frank managed to rescue him. This boy could have been killed if Frank did not think fast and rescue him. Frank's life was also in danger because some wanted to attack him but most respected him because they knew that he could fight. However, this boy was grateful that Frank saved his life. He requested Frank that they take a photo together so that he could show his family the boy who once saved his life at school.

Frank was a sad child at the same time who hardly laughed but unaware that his sadness was written all over his face. He remembered one day he was with some school friends after school they were just chatting and everybody giggling. There were some school girls not far from where they were standing and watching them.

When they decided to go one of those girls called him. They told him they were watching them chatting and everybody else was laughing and enjoying themselves in exception of him and he was not laughing at all. He told them that he thought he was also participating and was not aware that he was not laughing with everybody. He told them that there was nothing wrong with him and all along he thought he was laughing and enjoying the conversation like the rest of his friends.

As much as life was hard for Frank without his biological parents he forgot about them. It was like they did not exist and never existed whilst they were both alive. Although when his cousin sister was fetched by her mother he was wondering why his own mother could not do the same and fetches him to go and live with her.

CHAPTER 4

At some point Frank could not take it anymore, He was tired of being accused and get punished or being threatened with punishment. As they were living with many different relatives at home, there were those who would wrongly accuse him.

A certain relative accused him of disrespecting her and refusing when she instructs him to do anything for her. She also accused him of not wanting her to live in the house and that they should go and find a place of their own. A meeting was called and Frank's grandmother was present. Nevertheless Frank did not care anymore he came to a conclusion whatever they would say or do meant nothing to him. He was planning to run away from home and he was planning not to waste time and it was going to be the following day after the meeting.

It was the first time a meeting was called to resolve a problem involving him. Previously he would just be punished once and for all and everything would be over. On the night of the meeting Frank said nothing on his defense. This aunt who complained about him gave explanation of her complaint. For the first time his grandmother was very upset. She rejected her explanation as a fabricated story.

She told her if she wanted to move out of the house she should do so and not to make Frank as a scapegoat. As his grandmother raised him she knew what he was capable of doing and not. So it was easy for her to establish when lies are told about him.

She actually helped Frank to cancel his plans of escaping from home because he discovered that she really cared about him. That was the last time Frank was wrongly accused and he was never again punished since after that meeting. His aunt and his husband moved out of the house at last.

Frank worked hard at school fearing to fail and because his grandmother was struggling and could not afford to pay his school fees if he could repeat a class. His grandmother never went to school and she was working as a domestic worker. However, she was so passionate about education.

Frank's little cousin brother, Caesar was very intelligent and always full of jokes, vibrant and not reserved as Frank was. When their grandmother had cooked a chicken he would joke that he must be given the whole body because he was a visitor, their grandmother should dish for herself a head of the chicken because she was the head of the house.

Their little cousin sister to be given wings because she would fly away one day and Frank must be given the legs because he was the one who will be the pillar of the family. They used to laugh and their grandmother would ignore all those funny suggestions.

During Frank's final year at high school the year he wrote his matric his uncle passed away in that year. It was a sad moment for the whole family because it was least expected that he would die so soon because he was a very strong individual. He was a weight lifter and a body builder. Everybody did not think that he could just die just like that as he was not even that very old at the age of 45 years and was a very healthy person.

Frank's grandmother told Frank that his uncle had complained about stomach problems for some time before he died. She said she even suggested to him to get an African herbal medicines from traditional healers. Frank's uncle objected and told her that as a Christian he would not use such. It could be Frank's grandmother was worried about her son and her faith was tested because she was a Christian and did not believe in traditional healers.

She forgot that in (Psalms 50:15) the Lord says, "Call upon me on the day of trouble and I shall deliver thee and you shall glorify Me". Therefore, you do not seek help on something else you are not serving either than your God and your creator.

Frank's uncle had developed a strong faith that was the reason he objected in turning to traditional healers although his health was in danger. This was impressive as well because his uncle was not interested in Christianity before, except his gym. He used to train almost seven days a week.

Just few years before he passed on he completely changed and became a Christian. He changed in such a way that he would preach in the streets with his congregation. It was an amazing change and he did not care about his popularity or what people would say seeing him preaching in the streets.

Only his younger brother and two younger sisters were saved and were Christians before. However, his younger brother before he got saved he used to be an alcoholic but he also suddenly changed and served the Lord and had never looked back since then.

When Frank's uncle started to be seriously ill, he was admitted to a hospital and Frank was in boarding school by then. He got the news that he was in hospital from one of his school mates who visited home for few days and she knew Frank's family very well. She therefore went to see him in hospital and when she came back she told Frank that his uncle said she must pass his regards.

Frank was troubled about the news that he was in hospital, instead of thanking this girl of the message she gave him. He said to her he does not think that he would come out alive from hospital because he felt that there must be something very wrong happened to him. He has never been sick in his whole life since he knew him.

As Frank they were writing exams there were some days they got breaks and not writing. Frank decided to visit home one weekend. When he arrived at home he received the news that his uncle had died. Frank was really heartbroken about what he was just told and he wept and he was comforted by the family.

Frank listened to the explanation of his illness until the time arrived that he died. There was one lady who was also a relative. She was working as a professional nurse in the same hospital where he was admitted. She related an incident about him while he was still alive in hospital.

She said he was on drips and she arrived in his ward one day during his last days. He had removed the drips by himself she said she tried to put them back and asked him not to remove them. She said he responded that they should not waste their time with him because he was going. He asked her what time it was and that was the only thing he said most of the time she went to see him; he just wanted to know the time until eventually he was gone.

As much as Frank's uncle was harsh with him, he missed him. He felt his absence because he taught him a lot about discipline and self-defense against the thugs. He encouraged him to stay fit all the time by lifting weights, training karate and boxing. Frank was still training as he was taught and never stopped. He would wake up every morning and do rope skipping for thirty minutes, do pushups and about forty minutes he would do some weightlifting in his gym area at the basement of his house.

Sometimes when Frank was not going to work he would jog for about an hour and come back to finish up with pushups and bench-press. He did not have to go to a public gym as he had his own gym in the house and he would buy and add any extra equipment he required. All this was because of the training he received from his late uncle.

Despite all that, Frank discovered that he never let go of the hurt his uncle caused him. For many years he would dream having dreadful fights with him exchanging words with him although while he was still alive he never argued with him. It took him years having these kinds of dreams even after he was married with kids. He would still dream of his uncle and having heavy conflicts.

He managed to get over those dreams after he was a born again Christian and he prayed about them, that the Lord help him to remove that anger, un-forgiveness and resentment against his late uncle.

Chapter 5

After the funeral, Caesar and Nono spent most of their time at their late uncle's house. Frank stayed with their grandmother and he could notice that the passing on of her son had affected her so badly because she lost a lot of weight after the funeral and her health was not good. All of a sudden Frank was missing Caesar and Nono so much, it was like they had gone away to a faraway country and they have left him. Eventually Nono came back after a while but Caesar stayed at their uncle's house until Frank left Dundee, they were never together again since after the funeral.

Frank intended to go to university after he completed his matric using loan bursaries but his grandmother discouraged him. Thinking that although his school fees and books would be paid but he would not have money to buy clothes for himself and would not afford any other financial needs he would be faced with. She therefore suggested that he gets a job rather and work for few years and then go to tertiary. He took her advice but unfortunately he was lazy to go back to school. He ended up doing distance learning only after some years she had passed away.

He decided to go back to Benoni where he was born after finishing matric but he ended up living with relatives in Johannesburg. When he started to work he sent his grandmother money every month knowing that she was struggling. She was so grateful and blessed him a lot although he never visited her until after four years when he attended his little cousin's brother's funeral.

Caesar was murdered in the Free State after he had left school and was working as a credit control manager at a furniture store. The only little brother he had ever known had died in the most tragic manner in the hands of murderers who did not even know him. He was not a thug and was very decent and smut that those thugs could have taken away his life just like that.

They robbed Frank of the only little brother he had who used to understand and comfort him during the bleak moments of his life. The only person he knew as the only little brother he had, they shared the same pain in living. Like a wet soap he slipped away from his hands and like a smoke in the air he disappeared from his eyes. Frank never knew when he departed from Dundee that he will never see his brother again.

He never cried so much in all his life, he had many relatives who died before and after and he accepted their deaths but with Caesar it was very hard. He blamed himself because they never communicated much when he left school. He thought he could have put him aware that his life was not safe where he was and he could have done something.

Frank saw Caesar's clothes at the funeral which he was wearing before he was murdered they had blood stains although they had been washed and were torn because of the knives which were used in stabbing him.

The worse moment which knocked Frank down was when he saw his lifeless body in the casket his eyelashes had dry tears and there was soil on one of his cheeks. Frank started to have the imaginations of his last moments on this earth, the pain he went through being in the hands of merciless creatures and with no one around to help him. They were many and overpowered him. Some holding his arms from behind as Frank was told. He was powerless to fight and with no strength and because of the blood loss from the stabbing wounds he sustained from his attackers.

Frank was told that among the eight stabbing wounds he sustained the one which killed him. It was the result of the stabbing, cutting and damaging the main artery to the heart as they were gunning to stab his heart. Though none of those stabbing reached his heart but he could not make it.

Frank wept uncontrollable in despair, he was torn inside and angry against those who committed this crime against his little brother. There was a feeling of sombre as this was the moment of truth that he was really gone. After the funeral Frank sat with his grandmother and had a chat with her. The pain was clear in Frank's grandmother's eyes. She related to him that those thugs sent somebody whom he knew to lure him out from his house so that they could kill him. Frank tried to be strong as his grandmother was talking to him and also encouraged her to be strong thinking that this incident might affect her deteriorating life. The second day after the funeral Frank had to say goodbye to his family and he left going back to Johannesburg.

After some days after the funeral Frank and the family were advised of his little brother's court date. Frank left for the Free State with one of his friends. They found Frank's aunt who was his little cousin brother's mother and Frank's elder brother already there. They all went to court with some other relatives whom Caesar lived with. The court number they were given, they were told that it was not the one the case was supposed to be heard. The case was set in another court as an inquest.

They found an Afrikaans prosecutor in the inquest court, speaking in Afrikaans language he asked whether they were there (vir die saak van dooie man) for the case of a dead man. Those words opened the wounds which were trying to heal in Frank's heart. His little brother was now called a dead man. There was no sympathy in the way this man was talking. The life of a black person those days was worthless. Worse of all, the suspects were caught and arrested but all of a sudden the case was an inquest.

Frank knew immediately that extortion was paid and the investigating officer had tempered with the case to weaken it so that the accused should be discharged. How could a murder case be turned into an inquest while there were suspects who were arrested for the case and also there were state witnesses?

Frank could not find peace within himself he was broken and torn inside and had a big void in his heart and loneliness he felt. At the inquest court they were told that the case has been remanded for another date for hearing. Frank's aunt asked Frank what they should do next whether they should come to the next court date.

Frank suggested that they should just forget about that case if they did not want to be hurt anymore. As it was clear that there was no justice they were going to get in that whole matter but would bring back just all the bad memories. They agreed with him and they decided not to pursue that case anymore. His aunt and his big brother left the same day. Frank and his friend left the following day.

After the court case Frank requested to be taken to the place where his little brother was murdered. He was given a car and they left with three male relatives to show him the last place his brother was before he left this world. They arrived at the open veld and one of the relatives pointed to him the spot where he was lying until he died. Frank was quiet sitting in the car emotionless he did not come out of the vehicle. The tears were just running down his cheeks and he could not say anything except staring at the spot where he died. Eventually they tried to console him and suggested that they should go and they left.

Frank had some relief to see the last place where his brother was before he died. The following day Frank and his friend left for Johannesburg and they never got any information about what happened to that case, Frank was not sure whether he made a right suggestion that the family should forget about that case or not.

After that Frank was deeply hurt and did not care whether he could die. He once walked from one township to another from Meadowlands going home to Zondi very late in the evening. He did that because one of his uncles made me upset, this was a distance uncle. During that time there was a serial killer who was murdering people around these two areas Zondi and Meadowlands.

He arrived safe at home and he slept, after about an hour his uncle arrived and took him back. He told everybody that he found him sleeping at home. They could not believe that he walked home and yet people were being murdered by a serial killer. One of his uncle's friends was convinced that Frank was the serial killer because everybody was scared to walk at night especially for a long distance and yet Frank walked and for the fact that he was unharmed.

There was also another incident whereby Frank had to walk some girl who arrived at his house late and was scared to go home alone. Frank had to walk her to the nearby township where she lived. On the way they came across some thugs who were trying to stop passing vehicles and they were wielding knives. Frank was not scared of those thugs especially as he was upset having to walk this girl when he was supposed to be sleeping. He told himself if they could try him he will teach them a lesson. Very weird they did not even try to attack him instead they saluted him and opened the way that they should pass. It had registered to Frank when looking back at those incidences, He was convinced it was just the mercy of God and He protected him.

Frank continued being stubborn as a result of the hurt he suffered of the death of his brother, he developed a bad tendency of walking around late at night. One time he was from Naledi going home to Zondi on a Friday night but this time using a public transport. He went to a train station and there was a train which just left when he arrived. When he arrived at the platform he saw some group of people coming down and this gave him hope that there might be another train coming.

Unfortunately he was wrong because after this group of men arrived at the platform there were other three who jumped from the opposite platform coming to his direction. Then they had a conversation with the first group he saw coming down to the platform. Frank knew that something was not right there. He had some thoughts of seeing the newspaper with the headlines that a man was found murdered at the station.

These kinds of stories often appeared on daily newspapers. Anyway he did not have money with him and he was using a train ticket except his gold watch which was going to be the only valuable thing they could get from him. After chatting to each other they walked towards him. Frank was taught by his uncle in karate school that when being attacked by a group of people he must always identify the leader of the gang. So that you do not waste time with the rest you must defeat the leader and the rest would be history.

He identified the leader to be one of those who crossed from the opposite platform. He decided that he was going to attack first. He aimed to use a clenched fist and punched him in the lower jaw so that he could hurt this thug very hard but when he was close enough that he could attack. He hit him with an open hand in the face and it made a loud noise, as a result all of them dispersed and ran in different directions. He chased them and they jumped the railway line and disappeared.

Frank was not aware when he was chasing them that he had a company there was a gentleman who helped me in chasing them. This gentleman thanked Frank after they stopped because he felt he saved his life although Frank did not see him arriving. He told Frank that if he did not attack those thugs he was going to be next target after they had finished with Frank.

There were also other train commuters who were sitting on the opposite platform and they were applauding Frank because of the bravery he demonstrated by defeating armed men. Anyway when the train arrived they left and when Frank arrived at his station in Ikwezi station he said goodnight to his new friend and got off and his friend continued to the next station.

The last craziest thing Frank did because of the frustration of losing his little brother was to fight a man who was known of shooting and killing people and he was a policeman. For some foolish reasons he had a fight with him and he beat him. This man promised Frank that the fight was not over and he was going to pay heavy for what he did.

There was a group of friends which Frank used to transport by his uncle's mini bus. They had a social club every month coming together and would collect some certain amount of money which they would bank and share it at the end of the year. They first would have their meeting and after that it would be a party.

Frank attended this occasion again the following month after he had a fight with the cop and knew that cop would be there. Frank's cousin sisters tried to stop him not to go there because they heard about the incident but he was stubborn and went. When Frank arrived he was right at the gate and with few of his gang members. Frank could see they were in a mission of some sort. As he arrived everybody who knew Frank greeted him and he went inside the house and the cop and his gang followed him.

Inside lots of people were greeting and having conversation with Frank. He got himself a chair and sat down, he saw his rival turning back and saying to his friends "he is well known let's leave him" and they left. Frank would be fooling himself if he thought that man was afraid of him but he should know it was just of the mercy of God that he could not hurt him. He had the capacity to do so and he was with his gang members but for some reasons he could not.

Frank never saw that man again since that night he did not know what happened to him after that. Whether he was still alive but Frank regretted deeply that he fought him it was not necessary. He was not a threat to him before the fight he could have just walked away from him if he felt that he was irritating him. What Frank did was pure arrogant and foolish which he should be ashamed of himself.

CHAPTER 6

The following day Frank sat down and thought about all the dangers he went through and he realized the grace of God was upon him because also as a child he was knocked down by a truck riding a bicycle. It was at a stop sign he stopped next to a big truck and when it moved he also moved next to it on the left side of it but unfortunately it stopped because there was another small truck coming from the left side coming to their direction.

Frank did not see it because his view was obstructed by the truck he was riding next to. Obviously the other truck could not see him either. There was no way that this driver could have applied the brakes to avoid the accident. Frank thought to himself that it was over with his life and with a blink of an eye he was on top of the bonnet of this truck and from there he fell on the ground.

He stood up, only the bicycle was damaged and he was limping a bit. He never even went to hospital or to a doctor. When he arrived at home he told his grandmother and his uncle. His uncle was so excited thinking it was because of his trainings and Frank did a break-fall. However, Frank knew for sure that it was not because he used a break-fall to save his life but something supernatural saved his life.

Three years later after Frank's little brother had died, his grandmother passed away. Frank was already married with two boys. He went down to Dundee with his wife, his mother in-law and his two little sons. Frank was told that his grandmother suffered stroke before she died. She was in a comma for a while.

One of his aunts told him the last words his grandmother uttered before she was in a coma was calling Frank's name Miliki, which was his nick name and she never spoke again until she passed on. Frank's little cousin sister Nono was not there. Frank was told that it has been few years she disappeared and nobody knew where she was. This was also the same time he was told about his other cousin sister Deliwe who was married young and that she also had passed away.

It was just sad news after sad news. Frank sometimes wondered and asked himself whether the Lord allowed these things to happen that he ended up without siblings. He missed his grandmother, he thought about her a lot and how much she struggled to make sure they survive and had food on the table. That they also go to school and get educated and he realized how strong this old lady was.

Frank was also disappointed that his grandmother died before she could see his children because she had promised him to live until Frank had his own house and family.

Anyway when she died Frank had already these things but unfortunately she did not make it to see them.

As Frank was moving around with his big brother Joshua and other relatives preparing for the funeral, he was attracting a lot of attention wherever he goes in that small town. One could hear people mumbling asking one another who he was. Frank, Joshua and other relatives went to buy sheep at a certain farm. The farmer only enquired about Frank wanted to know where he was coming from. It was even worse when he was driving the car they used coming to the funeral. It was a hired new BMW 525i Frank's employer hired it for him. Everywhere they went people were steering at it. Those who had an opportunity to talk to Frank would tell him how beautiful his car was. At least these remarks made him to take a focus away from the fact that his grandmother has died.

Frank also met his former school mates they were all happy to see him again and they did their best after the funeral to host him. Frank and his family left for Johannesburg the following day everything went well except knowing that most of the people who were closed to him were gone because even his little cousin sister disappeared and no one knew her whereabouts.

Frank remembered the joke Caesar his little brother used to make when their grandmother had cooked a chicken. That their grandmother must dish for herself a head of the chicken as she was the head of the family. His brother demanded to be given the body of the chicken because he was a visitor, Nono to be given the wings because one day she was going to fly away and Frank to be given the legs as he was going to be the pillar of the family.

Like Frank's little brother prophesied he never stayed long in this world like a visitor he was gone forever. Frank's little sister flew away till this day she never came back and no one knew where she was, they had tried to look for her but with no success. Their grandmother also was gone as a head of the family she was there to raise them, lead them and leave.

Like a lonely pillar of the family Frank was left alone. He had lost also many of his distance cousins he grew up with after he left school who were also part of his family. The prophecy of Caesar was strong and so true. All these things he said jokingly came to pass and now Frank was left to tell the story. He had forgiven those who murdered his little brother.

After some months after the funeral Frank was told that his mother managed to get the message that her mother had died. She went down to Dundee to go and pay her last respect at the grave of her mother.

From Dundee, Frank was informed that she would like to go and spend some time with Frank's big brother Joshua in Bloemfontein and from there she would be coming to Johannesburg to spend time with Frank and his family. After visiting Frank, Frank was supposed to drive her to Nelspruit in Mpumalanga where she was now staying.

Frank was also advised that as per her mother's instructions he was not supposed to call her mom because where she was married both Frank and Joshua, were not known as her children. This was shocking news of another some sort of Frank's life. All the time he was under the impression that this woman was married to his father.

Frank felt very embarrassed because his wife was present when he was told of these instructions. Anyway there was little he could do about that because he did not choose to be born the way he was and be brought to this world and be treated the way he had been treated. He did not choose this ugly life and a mother who never raised him and at the end denied him as her son. However, Frank told himself that he was not going to collaborate and be the accomplice of those lies.

His mother arrived eventually at his house together with his sister in law. Frank's children were very young at the time. His wife introduced her to them as their grandmother although they never discussed with his wife how they were going to treat this situation. Even when his wife friends had visited she introduced her to them as Frank's mother.

There was not much Frank discussed with this woman as he did not know her and there was no bond between both of them as the mother and son. At the same time Frank was not bitter about anything that she never raised him and that she was denying him as her own biological son.

When the time arrived that Frank should take her back to Mpumalanga, he asked one of his distance cousins and one of his friends to accompany him going to Mpumalanga. They left with her in the morning around 10:00 am on a Saturday and arrived in the afternoon in Mpumalanga. They slept there and drove back the following day.

Before they left, there was an old woman from the neighbourhood who asked them who they were. Frank told her that the two gentlemen he was with were his cousins and that the woman of that house was his mother. He did that deliberately that there should be somebody who knows that his mother was hiding her other children which she had out of wedlock. He also told his three half-sisters and a half-brother that he was their brother and he let them know that they have an elder brother as well whose name was Joshua.

They exchanged phone numbers and they phoned each other now and then particularly with the elder one. As they communicated now and then with the elder sister, Frank asked her to ask his mother who his biological father was. She only told her his surname and did not tell her where he was or whether he was still alive or dead. This made Frank very upset and he decided that he will never again ask this woman about his father, she can keep that information until she dies without him having it.

Indeed his mother died eventually and he never got any details about his father. Frank just prayed to God for forgiveness if there be any resentments and un-forgiveness in his heart about his parents. He further thanked God for raising him and being his Father in all the days of his life and keeping His promise as He says in His Word that He will be the Father of the fatherless. Even if the father and mother can forsake their child He will not as it is stated in (Psalms 27:10) New King James version.

Frank thanked the Lord that he was the testimony of one of His promises. He had overcome many dangerous situations and survived and that was not by his power or might but it was by His Spirit.

Frank's brother and his uncle the younger brother of the one who passed way in Dundee and his aunt his mother's sister arrived at Frank's house the day before the funeral of his mother. They woke up very early in the morning the following day heading to Mpumalanga to the funeral. The funeral was early in the morning. They got lost because of the name changes of the roads by the new government in South Africa.

Frank tried to call his sisters but their phones were off as the funeral was in progress. At last when they switched on the cell phones he managed to speak to one of them. They were not very far from the place and they sent somebody to fetch them.

When they arrived the funeral was over and they were taken to her grave. As much as Frank's mother never raised him and never lived with her, there was sadness in Frank's heart of her death. In the afternoon they drove back to Johannesburg. His brother, his uncle and his aunt left immediately for their destination after they arrived at Frank's house.

CHAPTER 7

It had been always Frank's desire to leave South Africa for military training. As black people were oppressed and had no say and were treated with less respect and as third class citizens. This was something which bothered him a lot as a result he believed in the arm struggle as a kid raised in an apartheid country.

For some reasons things did not go right that he could leave the country. There were many young men who were arrested across the borders of South Africa at the time he wanted to leave. Therefore he was advised that it would not be possible for him to leave as he might get arrested. He was impatient and did not believe what those people were telling him. He decided that if he could not leave the country he was not going to continue fighting the struggle inside the country. He thought that he was too stubborn to fight the struggle inside the country and he could be easily killed by police.

He became inactive in the struggle and he stopped even attending the meetings. However, he was happy that he never crossed the country. He sincerely believed that he could have not survived because he did not even have a vision of what he wanted to do except got trained come and fight. He also thought it was the intervention of God that everything failed. When he looked back now many boys he knew who left the country most died. Even one of his second cousins he came back and did not live long and he died of some meningitis.

Frank decided to be ignorant of politics although it was not easy in South Africa as he got intimidated now and then. He fought every situation as it comes and he refused to be treated like nothing. He resisted any kind of humiliation laws. He thanked God again because he was never arrested. However, he could not stay away forever out of politics because after he bought his first house. He was recruited back to politics because many residents were losing their houses because they could not afford to pay bonds because of high interest rates or job losses.

Frank felt compelled to assist those residents who were struggling paying for their houses. By negotiating with the banks that they not be evicted and found a way that they continue paying what they could afford until they were in a position to pay the normal repayments. Therefore, he had to be a member of Soweto Civic Association so that the banks could listen to him. He was made a secretary of their branch in Chiawelo, Soweto.

He enjoyed this task because he helped many people to recover their houses. However, he discovered that it was not everyone who could not afford to pay their bonds because of financial problems, some misused their income. Like some men would spend their income on alcohol and failed to pay their bonds. Unfortunately the wives and their children would not be aware until the sheriff knocked at their doors.

This irresponsible behaviour used to frustrate him because children would be under the impression that they had a home only to be kicked out from that home because of the failure of their fathers to pay their bonds. Nevertheless in many situations Frank was the best negotiator and managed to save many families from eviction from their properties. One thing he used to enjoy was to put that smile back to the desperate families by resolving their bond problems.

In a certain case the husband was separating from his wife he then decided not to pay the repayments of his home loan until the bank decided to attach the property. This man left his family and gone to live with another woman, the poor wife was not earning enough to pay the house and with two sons who were still at school.

Not long after the husband has left them, there was an estate agent who was bringing people to come and view the house for purchasing. The woman brought the complaint to Frank's attention as a member of Civic Association. He advised this woman once this estate agent can bring other potential buyers to the house again she should send one of her sons to call him.

It was not long Frank was at home one Saturday afternoon. One of the boys came to alert him that the estate agent was at their house with people and a truck full load of household intending to occupy their house. Frank immediately rushed to their house and advised the boy at the meantime to go and call his other two comrades for him and that they should join him at the house.

When Frank arrived at the house the agent and the new owners of the house were there. He ignored the estate agent and spoke to the new owners of the house. He asked them where they were coming from and they told him. He enquired whether they have bought that property and they advised him that they did.

He then told them that there was a huge problem with the house they just bought as they could see that it was still occupied by people. While he was still talking his other two comrades arrived they caused some commotion and wanted to physically fight with the estate agent. Frank intervened and managed to stop them and he continued to explain the problem to the new owners of the house.

They were understanding and also indicated that they would not like to occupy a house which had problems. Frank told the estate agent that he would have to get them an alternative property. He told everybody the steps he was going to take that very same day he was going to write a letter to the bank and address it to the general manager and hand deliver it to the bank on Monday.

This procedure Frank was advised by one of the old Civic Association leaders who was working for the same bank which loaned the ex-husband of the lady to buy that house. He gave the people who were supposed to occupy the house his particulars and advised them that if this estate agent did not find them alternative property they should contact him and he was going to be in touch with the Civic Association of the place where they were coming from to solve their problem.

The new owners left although they were disappointed but they understood the problem they were faced with. When Frank arrived at home he immediately prepared the letter for the bank. On Monday morning he took it to the bank offices before he goes to work. It did not take him long to receive the reply. They confirmed the appointment he requested for a Saturday morning as he could not make it during the week as he was working.

On the day in question he went to the bank together with the lady he was trying to help. In the meeting with the general manager and two other managers they discussed the issue. It was discovered that the procedure was not followed before the house was attached. There was no communication sent to the occupants before it was finally sold.

The general manager decided to reverse the sale and also helped the other family who was buying that house to get them an alternative place. He further requested Frank to find out from the lady how she was intending to pay the house. She explained what she could afford.

It was agreed that she pays occupational rent of the money she could afford until she could afford to buy it back and pay the bond. This was more than fair and everybody was content with the decision and there were documents she was required to sign, Frank also signed as a witness. The meeting came to an end and they left. This lady was a Christian and she did not stop thanking God for Frank. She managed to buy back her house when one of her sons started to work. He helped his mother to settle the bond but Frank had left Soweto by then.

Even parents who had delinquent children Frank was called to assist and he did. He remembered one boy who was terrorising his mother and siblings with a fork spade, after Frank was called together with some of his comrades. This boy tried to attack Frank with the same fork spade he hit him once in the face with a clenched fist. He ran back where he took the spade and threw it away.

He never again gave his family problems he ended up being the sweetest boy in the family. He also had a high respect of Frank. Frank once drove past his old neighbourhood the father of that boy and other neighbours were standing in the street. They were delighted to see Frank again and this boy also came to greet him. He was not looking well. His father referred to Frank as the friend of his son and told him that his friend has been sick for a while but he was recovering.

In the meetings which the Civic Association used to hold during the week on Thursdays people would bring their different kinds of problems to the organisation seeking for solutions. There was also this one case which Frank also handled, two neighbours who were in conflict for years. They explained their case and the reasons they did not get along. Frank just felt not to waste time on this case. He told them to shake hands both families and let bygones be bygones. They shook hands, hug and cried. They apologised to each other for the unnecessary trauma they caused to each other and to their children.

This was awesome and a miracle, families who were in conflict for many years and they did not have to spend much time on resolving their case and they had such a breakthrough. Now something amusing whenever there was a similar case of neighbours who were in conflict. Some comrades wanted to apply the same strategy to solve their case. That could not work because Frank requested that should be done only in that particular case because he felt in his spirit to do so.

Frank had resigned from the Civic Association before he left Soweto because of some infighting for positions. He did not hide his reasons of resignation. He told them that he did not want to be identified with comrades who were fighting against each other for the sake of positions and yet their purpose was to help the community with problems. They tried to persuade him not to resign but he already made up his mind and he left them.

His concern of the infighting for power amongst the members of the organisation was confirmed, when one of the comrades, who was elected as a councillor refused to step down when his term of office had come to an end. It was almost after five years Frank was gone, a meeting was called by one of the senior members of ANC to resolve this problem. Frank also attended the meeting as he was around Soweto that day this was during the democratic government.

The leader from ANC explained the purpose of leadership within the organisation and the reasons why leaders need to leave the office and give others a chance to lead. He gave examples of leaders of ANC who came and left but the organisation continued to exist with different leadership. He further explained that leaders shall come and leaders shall go but the organisation shall always be there.

However, all this fell on deaf ears the Chiawelo branch was divided into two. There were those who were in favour of this council to stay a second term and those who wanted him to leave the office as his term had come to an end. Those who wanted him to stay were stronger and arrogant therefore they succeeded in keeping him against the constitution of the organisation and advices from the ANC.

The politics was now for money and most forgot that they joined politics to fight evil against the apartheid government and fighting for the poor and everybody to be free from oppression. Anyway greed spread like wild fire as well as the mother body ANC many leaders were just corrupt and serving for their own needs.

After Frank had left Soweto he would get messages from his former comrades that many residents were still enquiring about him. They wanted to know about his whereabouts and how he was doing.

Frank did not attend any church during those years he always thought that God will understand that they were oppressed and therefore they needed to free themselves before they can serve God. That was all wrong mentality he had because God was the One who freed them in South Africa. There was not much fighting they experienced that forced the apartheid government to surrender.

Deep down in his heart, Frank was not happy; there were times when he would wake up in the morning having a feeling that he was disobedient to his Father. He felt like he was not listening to Him and he was failing Him all the time. After the ANC government took over the country, he thought that there were no more excuses now for him; he had to serve his God. However, all that was just a thought but with no action until he felt that he was haunted by some evil spirits. He knew then that he was to seek the Lord because He was the only One who could save him.

He decided to go to church eventually this was his first step to have a relationship with the Lord. As he continued going to church he ended up being allowed to be laid hands to be confirmed for the next stage as he was one of the new members in the congregation. This church was not like the normal charismatic churches. It was one of those old religious churches which members wear a uniform.

During the process of laying hands there was an old woman who came to lay hands on Frank. The rest of the other new comers were also laid hands by different senior members of the church. It was a Saturday and the following day they had to come to church again as it was a Sunday. The old woman who laid hands on Frank was given an opportunity to share a testimony.

She told the congregation that as she was laying hands on Frank she saw a shepherd looking after sheep and was wearing white clothes facing opposite direction. From there he disappeared. She said she enquired where he went to but was not given an answer.

There was no further explanation and the story ended up like that. Frank continued going to church and attended a Bible study which was taking place in the mornings before church on Sundays. He eventually withdrew from this church because of some issues he did not agree with.

One of them which were bothering him most was the glorification of the senior pastor. People were ever thanking him for the great things which he did for them like healing, deliverance and blessings. Frank felt strongly in his spirit that only God does great things for humans and therefore only God was to be glorified. He decided to leave this church and also since things were not going well for him financially since he joined that church.

Frank just bought a new house and had left employment and he started a new business which was struggling to take off. He decided to drop this business and looked for employment and work again. He got employment and he was back in working for a boss again. There was somebody who was doing his garden at home. It was a man almost the same age with him just a year older than Frank.

One day he came to Frank and told him that he had a dream about him preaching to a group of people. This amazed Frank because it has been a while since he was not going to church and had never preached before. It also took him back during the time he was still a student at secondary school doing his first year.

They had an Afrikaans teacher who was coming from the Free State who spoke only Afrikaans and was very strict. All the students did not like this teacher particularly as he was teaching a subject which was not a favourite to everybody. Afrikaans was difficult and they all hated it as students they felt that it was forced to them to learn it.

This teacher came one morning for the period of his subject. He took all of them by surprise and said he wanted to tell them about a dream he had night before. The students were all inquisitive to hear his story as he was not a friendly person. He told them that his dream was about Frank. Frank was more curios wondering what was happening in this dream which involved him.

He said he dreamed of Frank being a priest, the whole class laughed at Frank. The reason they laughed it was because most teenagers then believed that it was not cool to be religious. Frank also laughed because it was the only thing he could do when other children were laughing at him. Deep down in his heart he was not laughing but surprised to learn that the Lord knows him and cared about him. The least important boy on earth who was rejected by both his parents at the most, tender age. He did not know that God would have anything to do with children who were not welcome in this world.

This was the second time for Frank as a school child that his teacher had dreamed about him. At primary school, the second school he went to his teacher also told the whole class that she had a dream about Frank. This time his teacher dreamed that he was getting married and there were wedding plans for him. She said she could not understand why at his age they allowed Frank to get married. Frank did not have any clue what that dream meant he just laughed as the whole class was laughing.

Frank's gardener also told him that he dreamed of him preaching to a group of people after so many years after he left school, this astonished him more. He felt now that he had an obligation to be obedient and serve the Lord and also serve His people. He continued to live a naïve life and not having an active relationship with God. However, he encouraged people to go to church and believe in God as He is the only solution for the problems of their lives. Even when he was nominated as a program director or as a speaker at funerals he preached the Word.

One day it was around dawn as it was the most period Frank had his dreams. He was asleep and he had a dream being inside a one room house. Which had a door which was cut in two halves, the upper door was opened. Suddenly there was a light flashing from the sky into this house.

He was filled with real fear even feared to look at this light. While he was still confused wondering what was happening he noticed that he was not alone in this house. He was in the company of a young boy who seemed not to take notice of what he was seeing. He enquired from him what was happening, he responded with less interest.

He told Frank that what he was seeing was exactly what Frank knew what it was and he was not even looking at Frank as he was busy fiddling with something in his hands. From there Frank woke up. He could still feel that light it was still so significant to him. As a result he decided that when he arrives at work he was going to ask one of the ladies who were Christians to direct him to a good Bible based church.

He did that and this lady directed him to a church somewhere in Kempton Park whose pastor was from Nigeria. Frank was not much comfortable to be amongst people he did not know but he had no choice he needed to be obedient to the Lord. One thing he feared was to keep on being stubborn and ended up in a tragic situation like a car accident. As he has heard that some stubborn people ended up in those situations before they could start to listen to the Lord and serve Him.

On his first arrival at that church there was a bishop from Ghana who was visiting and was preaching in that service. In finishing he encouraged people for the alter call. Frank raised his hand and went forward for the prayer. While he was standing there with the other people who came for the prayer. This bishop called his name but was not pronouncing it correctly. Frank lacked the courage to identify himself. The bishop even said he might not be pronouncing it correctly but still Frank did not respond.

So, Frank missed whatever message he was going to receive from that bishop. Now he was always praying to God that someday he will receive that message and he prayed for forgiveness for being disobedient because he made it appear that this poor bishop was just calling a name which did not exist. He has stayed in this church for a period of three years and this was the place where he learned to pray and fast.

They were fellowshipping in a rented office block and they were evicted after a year for rent defaulting. The pastor managed to organise a temporary venue while the church was still trying to get its own place. While they were still at this temporary place the pastor requested Frank every morning to take music instruments from his residence to the church and back to his place after the church.

Frank had a Jeep Grand Cherokee which was big enough to assist with this task. After the church got its own permanent venue he did not have to take the instruments to and fro anymore. He appreciated the period he spent in this church because he grew spiritually and understood the Scriptures better. Although it was a place he did not know anybody he was accepted as part of the family.

He left after he finished three years, his pastor was sad he thought maybe he was leaving because he was not happy about something. He told Frank he fasted and prayed to the Lord that he should come back and he apologised to him if he did anything wrong to him. He also asked other pastors of the church to speak to Frank. Frank told his pastor that there was nothing wrong he did. He explained to him that he was at his church for a purpose and he had learned a lot and he needed to move on after that. Frank assured him that he will visit whenever he had a chance.

The original name of this church was "Camp David"; however, the pastor changed it at a later stage. The meaning of the original name was a place of learning and Frank did learn a lot and he could not stay longer. The pastor accepted his explanation although Frank could see he was still not happy but there was not much he could do to stop him.

Frank left and went to join another church which was based in Soweto and had a satellite church in Kempton Park. He attended the satellite one in Kempton Park because it was nearer for him from his house. The advantage about this church they had home cell groups which Frank felt he needed for his growing spiritually.

He needed that discussion with the fellow believers and giving of testimonies and asking of questions. In a big church sometimes one feels lost when there are no home cells. He was given an opportunity to preach now and then. Most of the members of his group used to like Frank they nicknamed him the preacher.

CHAPTER 8

Frank told his friends that he was now a born again Christian. He deliberately used those specific words so that they should lose interest in him as their friend and reject him. In most cases with the unbelievers in his country they regarded the born again Christians as crazy people who were confused. Frank did not want to say to them he could not be their friend anymore because he lived a different life. He wanted that it should be them who reject him so that he could not feel guilty that he left them. They all laughed at him.

He consistently attended the church services and he visited his friends on Sundays after church. They would ask whether he went to church and he would tell them that he did all the time.

At some stage it was not easy for him to go to the South African indigenous churches as there were few men. As men in South Africa had a concept that church was for women. They believed that men should remain manly. Therefore when you start to talk about church or attending church services that means you are weak and you are acting like women.

One thing which encouraged Frank to continue going to church was that he convinced himself if God wanted him to be in the church he had to do it irrespective how he felt. He was convinced that it was no more about him anymore and it was about Jesus whom he has agreed to serve.

At last his friends also began to have an interest and wanted to go with him to church. It looked like he won their hearts but they were lazy to wake up in the mornings whenever he had an appointment with them to go to church. One of them managed to wake up one morning and they went together. He was very impressed and he would go even without Frank. As a result he ended accepting Jesus as his personal saver.

Frank's life completely changed he took many people who knew him by surprise. Some were convinced that he was dying and that was the reason he decided to change and have a relationship with God. There were different kinds of suggestions some just to make him feel guilty and be discouraged.

Some were good like one close relative of his who was also his friend said he knew what was going on with Frank and that he had a calling. It was interesting to Frank to hear this statement because his friend was not a Christian but he knew about a calling. Frank occasionally used to take alcohol and now he completely stopped and not even took a taste of champagne for a toast on celebrations. It just happened that he stopped taking alcohol not that somebody advised him to do so.

At home if he wanted to watch television, it was only Christian channels like TBN and Christian music. He lost interest even to listen or watch news there was nothing special about news that interested him anymore. Some would regard him as paranoid schizophrenia. He was eager to learn more about things which were related to Christianity. He found peace in reading the Bible and praying, he started to have less stress about useless aspects of life which used to frustrate him.

In companies he worked for he represented many employees who found themselves on the wrong side of the company's law. Many people would not want to get involved with anybody who was in trouble for breaking the rules of the company. So the reason which compelled Frank to be on the side of these employees was to help them as they found themselves alone in the most challenging time of their life.

He wanted them to get fair hearings and not feel intimidated and be afraid in stating and defending their cases. As well as his former colleagues would phone him when they found themselves in trouble in their new employment and would seek advice from him. Frank paid a price as well in representing the others because every choice you take in life goes with a price.

He had been stagnated in one position but he was fine with that than to betray people for the sake of going up the ladder. Since before he was born again Christian he knew the Bible in (Exodus 20:16) King James Version that you shall not bear false witness against your neighbour. In cases where he was instructed to issue written warnings against staff members. He would first investigate the case if he could find a person being innocent he would refuse to give such warnings.

Another reason he also once went through a hearing procedure being an accused person therefore he knew how stressful and scary it was, particularly if you have never been exposed to such a procedure. With the assistance he gave the workers they had confidence and stated their cases without fear.

In his case one of his bosses put him through it. He was a new boss and was given an instruction to get rid of Frank. He fell into a trap signing a timesheet of a temporary worker. It was on a Monday and he told him that the person he was reporting to was not available. Frank did go and check and could not find his boss but he did not check that this staff member had claimed for working the past weekend and yet he did not work.

It just did not cross his mind that he was up to mischief Frank signed his time sheet. That was a big issue and he was advised that he was going to be put on disciplinary hearing. It did not take place immediately. Only after three months the date was set, it could be they did that just to frustrate him because it was not nice knowing that there is a pending case against you.

They would send him emails just to remind him about the case. This was stressful for Frank when he thought that they might have decided not to continue with the case. He had to pray and fast because he did not have a plan B that if he loses his job what he would do. When the date arrived it was long overdue he just wanted to deal and get over with this case whatever outcome.

The management had well prepared their case with documents of exhibits and three witnesses. It was like a war between David and Goliath. Goliath a giant and well-built and had a bronze helmet on his head and he was armed with a coat of mail and the weight of his coat was five thousand shekels of bronze.

He had bronze armour on his legs and bronze javelin between his shoulders. Now the staff of his spear was like a weaver's beam and his iron spearhead weighed six hundred shekels (1Samuel 17:4-7) King James Version. This is how Frank could describe how prepared the management were with their case.

Like David using a sling and five stones. Frank had only the charge sheet which was given to him explaining the charges against him. One lady from Human Resources who saw him was very worried she quickly organised a writing pad and a pen. She even reminded him that he must not be quiet and he must defend himself. Frank promised her that he will do so.

During the proceedings Frank's boss as a complainant was sitting next to him. Frank noticed that he was shivering like he was feeling very cold in a most freezing cold winter. This was amazing because Frank was supposed to be the one who shivered as his job was on the line. Frank never used the writing pad that was supplied by HR to him. His boss read his evidence and supplied everyone with the exhibits he prepared.

When he finished reading he told Frank that it was his turn to talk, Frank told him that it was not him who will tell him when to talk only the presiding officer will advise him. You could have seen in his face that he was upset about what Frank just said. The presiding officer gave Frank an opportunity to cross examine his evidence. He asked him one question and he explained something else which was irrelevant to his question. Frank told him that his answer was not relevant to what he just asked him and he made an embarrassment of him.

There were also some few other questions he asked him but his response was not that good. That gave Frank an impression that he did not prepare his case well as he had assumed. He was then allowed to call his witnesses. His first witness was an employment agent of the temp staff who put Frank in that trouble. His major evidence was that this staff member informed him that he made Frank to sign his timesheet with intent to commit fraud and he knew Frank was the softest person in management and would not take notice of his intentions.

When he finished with his evidence Frank told the chairperson that he was objecting to that witness's evidence because it was hear say. He said the person who was making allegations about him was supposed to be present in the hearing and give evidence himself. Frank's objection was sustained and the evidence of this witness was rejected. Two more witnesses were called Frank only asked them one same question each and they agreed with him unaware they were throwing their case. The last one tried to resist answering his question. He told Frank that he was not the one who was on trial. It was obvious he had a wrong impression that if you are not on trial you cannot be grilled with questions.

When they all had finished Frank requested to give his evidence. He made it sure that it was not long and he was brief to the point. The complainant never cross examined his evidence to discredit it. That was the biggest mistake in all other mistakes they made because that was like whatever Frank said he agreed with him.

The case was remanded for about a week. When they returned the chairperson found Frank not guilty on all the charges which were laid against him. He explained his reasons that the two witnesses of the complainant collaborated with Frank in cross examination. The complainant failed to cross examine Frank's evidence therefore, his case was found to be flawed.

Most of Frank's colleagues were comfortable talking to him about anything which was affecting their life. They would feel better after they had a discussion with Frank and they would beg him that he should never change even if he could be pressurised. Frank also encouraged many to accept Jesus for their salvation.

There was one incident which kept on coming back on Frank mind. One of his colleagues arrived at work one Friday she was on late shift. Frank stood up from his desk she was about ten paces from where he was. He screamed at her wanting to find out from her whether she would accept Jesus Christ as her personal saver so that when she dies she would know where her soul would go.

Before she could answer there was one lady who was a born again Christian and she was her friend and she replied that she was saved and she does go to church. Frank yelled at her to shut up as he was not talking to her. She immediately kept quiet seeing the seriousness from his face. The lady he was talking to responded and said yes I accept Jesus.

Frank calmed down and said thank you to her and he sat down. What triggered this kind of behaviour with him, he also did not know, the following week Frank was on study leave for few days. He never saw that lady the whole day of that incident and on Monday he was on study leave.

On Tuesday while Frank was busy studying preparing for exams, his boss called him on the phone. He informed him that the lady in question has died. She was gunned down by her husband on Monday morning while she was preparing to go to work. This was sad news but at the same time Frank had full hope that she was in heaven when he remembered his rude conversation with her. Frank believed that Holy Spirit spoke through him to her.

From there Frank received many calls from his colleagues most remembering his conversation with her. One gentleman in management even suggested that Frank must finish studying his course and be a counsellor and help people.

CHAPTER 9

It has not been an easy path for Frank the path he took. Christians with their Christian masks were not as holy as he has always thought. People were not treated equal because those who were not of high profile were not much recognised in the church than celebrities or those who occupied high positions in the government departments.

Also from most communities the foreign pastors and their churches were not accepted. People would complain that these pastors were disguising with religion and their main motive was drug trafficking. These were serious allegations to speculate about with no proof.

It was wrong as Christians to stand on God's way by discrediting those who accepted His calling. God sends evangelists, missionaries and pastors in different parts of the world for His purpose and if other Christians persecute these men because of their wrong reasons. They were persecuting God Himself.

At the same time Frank was aware that it would be ignorant to say that there were not those who came to the country with wrong motives. However, that did not give everyone a right as Christians to label everybody coming from Nigeria as a criminal.

Some would even further argue that they were misleading the youth and their preaching was not Bible based. They would talk about churches which mushroomed from nowhere. One would not have a problem if people were raising concerns about valid reasons. At the same time, it was important to guard the youth not to be misled. It was also important that if one was suspicious of something that he does some investigations before one can come up with suggestions.

So in this case what Frank discovered about those people who were criticising the new churches they had never tried to investigate their suspicions. Frank had actually did pay some visits to some of those Nigerian churches and found that whatever preaching taking place was biblical. They did not compromise the Bible and were raising issues which most of those old South African indigenous churches were ignoring from the Bible.

Instead Frank found that parents and the so called old churches were failing the youth because the youth was expected to be perfect without guidance. If you fail to teach and guide your children in the way you want them to grow, somebody out there will take over and teach them what they want to teach them.

Like there were many young people who were heavy on drugs, alcohol abuse and violence. Some were involved in Satanism because very few genuine adults had time to talk to those kids and understand their problems. No one saw the need to educate and motivate the youth regarding the meaning and importance of having a biblical worldview.

The Bible reflects the realities of everyday life over a long period of time and in many different social and historical contexts. From the Old Testament when God wanted to address His people He would instruct Moses to gather them and included women and children.

Like when the Israelites were afraid to take possession of the Promised Land, after they heard that people who lived there were huge and strong and could not be conquered. They wanted to go back to Egypt the land of their slavery. God intervened and told them He would give them their wish and they would not enter the Promised Land. However, He would took the younger generation including children and lead them to possess the land.

In this generation there would be no younger generation to take from as they have been neglected and condemned as a lost generation. Jesus said as well that the kingdom of heaven belongs to the little ones (Luke 18:16) King James Version.

In (Mathew 18:6) Jesus further says, "But whoever causes one of these little ones who believe in Me to sin, it would be better for him if a millstone were hung around his neck and he were drowned in the depth of the sea." Therefore, it was not understandable why people would cause grief to the youth of that era and ignore what the Bible teaches.

The children were criticised as well when they attended church and told that those churches of foreign nationals gave them wrong teachings. To come to the defence of those children one would refer life as a relay race. In a relay if you fail to hand over the baton to a next runner you lose the race. In South Africa it seemed like the race had been lost because parents failed to hand over the baton to the next runner.

As the youth was labelled as the lost generation one might agree on that point but the parents were to be blamed. As it was a common cause if you fail to give directions to somebody whom you want that they should take they will be lost obviously.

Therefore if parents failed to teach their children between right and wrong or about God they could not expect them to know that. Parents were also taught as children and it was surprising how now they could not teach their children.

Parents were expected to be the bridges for their children to cross over to the other side. They were not supposed to be shaky bridges which were not secured for crossing. Like bridges which look strong on the surface and yet underneath were corroded and damaged and dangerous to use. Until they took action they were still going to continue to complain about their youth.

Further, the Scripture needed to be read as in (Matthew 28:16-20) says, "The great Commission", Jesus had sent the eleven disciples to Galilee, to the mountain which He had appointed them. He instructed them to make disciples of all the nations, baptizing them in the name of the Father and the Son and the Holy Spirit.

Teaching the people to observe all things that Jesus had commanded them and to spread the Gospel up to the ends of the earth; therefore, these pastors from foreign nationals have adhered to the calling of Jesus Christ. Most it was not by choice to be in any country and did what they were doing.

Another problem black South Africans did not cross borders to do missionary work that was the reason they did not understand the presence of pastors from other countries. It was paramount that South African black Christians were taught about the missionary work. That they get involved in missionary and not only necessarily cross the borders but get deployed in the rural areas of South Africa where the Gospel had not been found and spread it.

They could also help financially to those missionaries who were out there in the poor and dangerous areas of Africa. They could also pray for them to be protected in all kinds of dangers. By so doing they could play a big role in contributing that the missionary work could stay active and many people be saved where there was no means that they could get the salvation.

As Frank was growing in Christianity he had also investigated the existence of ancestors. As in South Africa and in the black community many strongly believed in ancestors. There were rituals which were conducted like slaughtering of goats or cattle and other animals irrespective how educated were the families.

This was most common and sensitive practice to challenge and a deep concern for Frank because in some cases relatives and friends would regard you as a lunatic when you reject ancestors. One of the problems which Frank believed encouraged the unbelievers that this custom not to be abandoned.

The Christians failed to give proper explanation of their objections to the ancestral beliefs. Some Christians practised those rituals too in black communities and believed that ancestors were nearer to God and they could negotiate on their behalf.

Ignoring the fact that only Jesus Christ was the advocate and He died for everyone who believes in Him and was resurrected on the third day. He redeemed the believers through His crucifixion and only through Him one can go to the Father.

Most of the unbelievers believed that the rituals of animals were biblical and it was in the Old Testament. When one could ask for the reference in the Bible but no one could ever advise. Sometimes one would be told that Israelites used to do the rituals.

One would agree with that point but the Israelites were doing those sacrifices for God. They did burn sacrifices for God until Jesus Christ was crucified and there was no more sacrifices needed because He had been the atonement for the believers. At the same time Israelites did not sacrifice for the dead.

God warns in Deuteronomy 18:11 King James Version that one should not call upon the dead. The Lord does not just warn that the dead must not be contacted. This is for the protection of the people because the dead are not contactable but one will end up dealing with demonic spirits who pretend to be the ancestors.

When you do rituals for the ancestors with the animals either goats or cattle, the blood of sacrifice goes to these familiar spirits. This takes Frank back to the time he saw creatures when he was still a child after the ritual was done. Surely the Lord wanted Frank to know about those demons although he was still very young and He kept his memory to remember from that young age.

This was a tough issue indeed with the black community. It needed a lot of prayer that God could give a revelation to the people that they could be able to know that they were playing in the backyard of the devil by those animal sacrifices. It was a common thing when an individual received a miracle and they would comment that their ancestors have blessed them.

Also in situations when a person was ill and not becoming better, they consulted with traditional healers for a remedy. As much as it is stipulated in the Bible in (Leviticus 19:31) New King James Version that, one must give no regard to mediums and familiar spirits; do not seek after them to be defiled by them.

Not only that those traditional healers would fail to heal an individual but they were defiling the body and soul of the individual but people still went to them. A good example which they were supposed to take note of was the most expensive car like Ferrari when it needed a service or having a breakdown. You would not take it to a backyard mechanic in the township but you take it to a dealer of Ferrari.

So, the question would be why then in human situation when a person was sick would not seek help from God the one who created human beings. The One who knows human beings from the crown of their heads to the bottom of their feet? God is the one who can detect and heal any kind of sickness and diseases.

If not immediately praying consult a professional doctor who studied the body of human being and sicknesses which affect the body and the health of a human being.

One should be proud of contacting the Lord about such problems as one was proud of taking their expensive cars to the big names of manufacturers of those vehicles. Therefore you should actually be more proud as you could not compare Him with anything in existence as He is the creator of existence.

CHAPTER 10

After some few years Frank's brother in law was carjacked at a gun point. It was at night just after 08:00pm at his driveway when he went to open the gate to park his vehicle. Another vehicle from nowhere parked behind him and one of the occupants came out and pointed a gun at him. He instructed him to hand over his car keys or else he would blow his head off.

He handed over the keys and from there they searched him and took his wallet and every valuable thing which they could find in his possession and they left. This was a second time he was robbed of a vehicle at his driveway. When Frank heard the news he was troubled because it was not long he had been retrenched from work and was still paying back bank finance for his car.

The first carjack although Frank felt sorry for him but at least he was still working and the car was insured. With the recent one Frank was worried that he would be paying a car which he did not own anymore. He arranged a meeting with him so that he could see how he could help him. When Frank met him he told him that the insurance he had was a group cover, arranged by his employer.

Frank advised him to claim the insurance and it should be the insurers who repudiate the claim if the policy had lapsed. He definitely did and he was advised to contact his employer as the policy was a group cover arranged by the employer. He contacted the employer and explained the situation to them but they rejected his request and advise him that he was no more insured.

After his request was rejected Frank asked him to get him the name and email address of the highest person in his former employment. Frank sent him an email and stated his case they phoned Frank's brother in law requesting to see him. He went to see them but there was no help they offered him except an apology and advised him that there was nothing they could do as his vehicle was no more on the cover of the company.

Frank told his brother in law that they could pursue the case with his former employer by getting an attorney to fight for him but that would cost him money and he will not have enough as he was unemployed.

He told him that he was going to pray and he needed his faith in God that they could be able to recover his vehicle. Frank knew his brother in law believed in mediums so he told him he can only pray if he assured him that he was not going to involve any mediums to recover his car. He promised that he will only have faith in the Lord the true God who created heaven and earth.

Frank was encouraged to hear of his faith and the first thing he did before his prayer he started by fasting. He remembered when David was allied with the Philistines running away from Saul and harboured by Achish the son of Maoch, king of Gath (1Samuel 27:2) New King James Version. When the Philistines were at war with Saul and Israel Achish instructed David to go with him to the war and fight Israel on his side (1Samuel 28:1) New King James Version.

Fortunately for David he was saved from this battle by being rejected by the princes of Philistines because they did not trust David that he might turn against them in the war since himself he was an Israelite. Achish allowed David to go back home with his men.

On the third day when David and his men arrived at Ziklag they discovered that the Amalekites had invaded the South and Ziklag. They had taken captive the women and children and those who were there and carried them away (1Samuel 30:2).

So David enquired of the Lord, saying. "Shall I pursue this troop? Shall I overtake them?" The Lord answered him and said, "Pursue, for you shall surely overtake them and without fail recover all."

Frank cried out to the Lord on behalf of his brother in law as David did that they overtake these criminals and recover his brother in law's vehicle without being damaged. Now and then Frank visited his brother in law so that he should not feel devastated and he assured him that he was with him and the Lord was going to help them to find his car.

After about three months after still nothing was happening and no sign of the vehicle. When Frank phoned his brother in law during the day his cell phone would be switched off. Frank suspected that he might be consulting the mediums. He enquired from his wife and his wife confirmed that it was true he has been seeing some traditional doctor.

This confirmed his suspicion and this was a typical example of black South Africans who were unbelievers. They could assure you that they do not believe or consult mediums but when they were out of the sight of people who knew them they sneak to these mediums like Saul when he could not hear any more from the Lord. Same applies when they were in tribulations they would slaughter an animal for sacrifice to the ancestors.

Frank called him one evening very upset and told him to count him out from his problems. He told him he can continue seeking help from his mediums and on his side he was cancelling praying for him. He begged him to continue praying because he needed his car and he will not go back to his witchdoctor.

He told Frank that this witchdoctor told him that he was going to find his car after three days from the first day he consulted him and it has been months since then and nothing was happening and he has paid him a lot of money. Frank told him that was not his problem anymore and he can sort that with him. He told him if he trusted in God he was supposed to trust unto Him only and don't mix Him with witchcraft. He promised to withdraw his consultation with the medium.

Frank agreed to continue praying on condition that he never again goes back to his witchdoctor and if he could find out he was still consulting with witchcraft he would withdraw without letting him. He promised he was going to be faithful to the Lord and Frank continued praying having faith that the car will be recovered.

After seven months his brother in law received a call from the police station of New Castle in Kwa-Zulu Natal. He was told to come and identify his vehicle and to bring together the spare key and together with the registration documents of the vehicle. He did not inform Frank immediately he first phoned his younger brother and his cousin brother to help him to fetch the car.

After they let him down he contacted Frank and Frank agreed. He woke up very early in the morning the following day and drove him to the place. They arrived in New Cattle in the midday and did all the paperwork needed and they were taken to the police premises where the car was kept. One policeman told his brother in law that he was fortunate that his car was found because from his experience the hijacked cars were not likely to be recovered.

Frank said it was because of the grace of God, this policeman replied that it was only because of the ancestors of his brother in law that his car had been recovered. Frank decided not going to argue this point and it was up to his brother in law to believe what he wanted to believe. Frank thanked the Lord that He did not let them down.

They were directed to the engineers to take the car to change the engine and body numbers back to the original ones as they were tempered with, also engrave the police clearance number which would show that the car was stolen and recovered. After all that was done they drove back to Johannesburg in late afternoon and arrived home safely very late in the evening.

At least one thing Frank appreciated about his brother in law. He told him that one of his friends had advised him to go to any church and make an offering of any amount of money which he could afford to thank the Lord. He said he did that and he made the offering.

That was the best thing to do than slaughtering a goat to thank the ancestors as this was the norm with most people in the community. It happened once when Frank helped one family from losing their house in Soweto. After the bank had agreed not to attach it, Frank was with his comrades just a while after the case. They invited them in an ancestral ritual for thanks giving. They promised to go but never attended.

Frankly nobody develops his worldview within a social vacuum. It is mostly constructed within the context of culture, information, practices and conditions that provide meaning and identity to a group of people.

People have a choice to follow whatever they wish to follow and practise; however, God created the whole living beings and the entire universe and it is proper to follow His culture.

As (Genesis 1:1) New King James Version says, "In the beginning God created the heavens and the earth."

Before God began to create the universe, nothing existed except God Himself. In Latin phrase "ex nihilo" out of nothing He created the universe. In (John 1:3) New King James Version says, "All things were made through Him and without Him was not anything made that was made."

By these explanations the main aim was to get into the reason behind most of the black people started to have these ancestral beliefs. The creation of the entire universe includes the creation of an unseen, spiritual realm of existence. God created the angels and other kinds of heavenly beings as well as animals and human beings.

(Revelation 10:6) New King James Version confirms that God did not only create the earth but also heaven and what is in it. Like (Colossians 1:16) New King James Version explains that, "For by Him all things were created that are in heaven and that are on earth, visible and invisible, whether thrones or dominions or principalities or powers. All things were created through Him and for Him."

The Western community do not have much consideration of spiritual realm and the influence of spirit beings and therefore may play little part in their daily thinking. This is being the reason that secular West does not believe in spirits. The devil's achievement in this part of the world was to convince them that he does not exist.

Like Christians who are from the West, are influenced by its materialistic outlook, believe intellectually in the spirit world, however, practically in most cases they live as if it is not real. In contras Africans are profoundly aware of the spirit world. They know that spirits exist in real and they experience their power.

They believe that spiritual forces have an influence in their lives and they do not have a difference of life into sacred and secular. A person raised in a traditional African community will likely be acutely aware of the spirit world although they may not always interpret it from a biblical understanding.

These spirits are demons which were fallen angels who rebelled against God. The devil is the leader of the demons, following Scriptures confirmation in (2 Peter 2:4; Jude 6 & Revelation 12:7-9) New King James Version. Now these demonic or evil spirits, in most cases in African community impersonate the deceased human beings and act as ancestors to the Africans.

That is the reason many Africans believe that deceased human beings continue to live as disembodied spirits, interacting with the living and influencing their lives. This view is unscriptural. As the Bible, teaches that when human beings die, their spirit separate from their body and it goes either to heaven or to hell depending on their standing before God. After death human beings can neither communicate with the living nor influence life on earth.

All such contact is with demons posing as relatives, using their advanced knowledge of human beings to impersonate the dead relatives. Demons respond to attempts to contact deceased relatives because it gives Satan an opportunity to gain control over people's minds and souls.

It is the duty of the churches to start to preach the truth as it is written in the Bible to take the people out of this darkness. There is no Scripture which is only for the black Africans. The Bible is one and it gives same message to everybody irrespective of colour or creed.

Frank once had a discussion with one of his nephews talking about these ancestral sacrifices. Frank's nephew told him that he should remember that they were black people, Frank asked him to show him any Scripture which was related only to black people. He told him that the Bible says that one should honour his parents so that it may go well with him and that he may live long.

Frank told him that he agrees with him it is true but the Scripture has got nothing to do with the ancestral sacrifices. He said if they are deceased they need to do rituals for them. Frank told him that was a lie there is nothing like that in the Scripture. He promised to get Frank that Scripture and will let him know. Unfortunately he had passed away after suffering from HIV/AIDS before he could come back to Frank with the Scripture.

What he told Frank was clear that he must have been taught from somewhere and that could have been from the church he used to attend. One of those old religious churches which has been indoctrinating people with wrong perceptions for years.

Frank had hoped that his nephew was going to be with him longer and have enough time to debate with him. What was good about him as much as he loved and respected Frank but he was not afraid to defend his faith and challenged him unfortunately it was a wrong faith.

Frank had the perception that his nephew was going to live for a long time since both his parents died and he was left with his younger sister. He forgot the fact that Satan does not stop to steal and to destroy and he does not rest to do evil. As long as he gets an opportunity he uses it whether young or old.

As Jesus warned in (John 10:10) New King James Version that, "The thief does not come except to steal and kill and to destroy, I have come that they may have life and that they may have it more abundantly."

A distance cousin sister of Frank was married in Durban with two children a boy and a girl. The boy was the eldest child in the family and was the one Frank used to have those debates. Frank's nephew lost his father first, during the uprisings just before the first democratic elections took place in South Africa. There was a third force, which was instigating violence and killings amongst blacks just to destabilise the country.

A political party which was called Iqembu Party was used mainly to commit these atrocities. This party would attack anybody who was not their member and kill them irrespective that they were not affiliated to any political party. This group believed if you were not their member you belonged to ANC.

They were a group of illiterate people although their leader was highly educated and was used by the previous government against anyone who opposed their system. One Saturday afternoon this group of people attacked the residents of one of the townships in Durban where Frank's nephew and his parents used to live.

Frank's nephew's father refused that day to flee as they used to do as men since they were the main targets. He instructed his wife to lock him inside the house together with his son as they could be attacked if found by these people. Unfortunately when these hooligans arrived they demanded that the door be unlocked. The wife had to do as instructed otherwise she could have been killed.

After the door was opened they found Frank's cousin sister's husband and his nephew inside the house. They shot and killed him in front of his son fortunately they did not kill the boy. Frank was always concerned about his nephew that incident was going to affect him negatively in life as he was growing but he was fine.

After the funeral they relocated to Johannesburg. This boy was a hard worker he would help his mother financially by washing taxi vehicles and the money he received he gave it to his mother. His mother phoned and complained to Frank about that. Frank went to speak to his nephew to refrain from washing taxis but he reasoned with Frank that he was only helping his mother as she was struggling financially.

Two years after democracy black people were still struggling financially. Frank's cousin sister joined politics and was affiliated to one of the opposition parties to the ANC. One day she phoned Frank, it was on a Wednesday to inform him that they were going to travel to Cape Town attending a parliament meeting as the members of the opposition.

She told him that they were going to travel by a mini bus. Frank was a bit sceptical of the mode of transport they were going to use as there were many road accidents particularly caused by mini buses at the time. He tried not to be negative and agreed with her to go on the trip. She promised to call him back the following week when they were back from Cape Town.

On a Friday morning the very same week Frank received a call from a male voice with an Afrikaans accent at work. He asked him whether he knew Evelyn Vilakazi and that was Frank's cousin sister. He wanted to know how he was related to her, Frank explained to him. After his explanation he told him that person had been killed in a car accident.

Frank just went blank for a while and could not respond. It sounded like a bad dream and was like he was going to wake up from it but it was not a dream it was real she was dead. After he regained consciousness, this gentleman told him that he would be in touch with him now and then for funeral arrangements.

Frank advised his boss at work and he left to go and alert the family and the deceased's mother. It was after a year Frank had been not visiting his relatives and there he arrived bringing bad news for them. After the whole family had gathered together he was instructed to fetch the children from school his nephew and his niece.

Frank went to his niece's school first and he informed the principal. They were all in great shock and they let her go with him and she was just crying all the way. Later Frank fetched his nephew he did not tell him until he arrived at home and he was told what happened. He also cried for losing his mother.

He then requested to speak to Frank alone. They went outside and he told Frank that his mother had advised him that if she could die they should take Frank as their next of kin. Any problems they might have which needed a parent they should speak to Frank. Frank told him that he does not have a problem with that and he will honour his mother's wish.

Frank was at the same time happy to see that his nephew was fine after hearing about his mother's death because he thought he was going to be devastated. The funeral arrangements were made and they buried his cousin sister the following week. Frank helped them to claim their mother's insurance policies and pension fund from her employer.

Frank's nephew updated him about any new developments which were affecting their lives. After he finished school he bought a mini bus and used it for a taxi business. His nephew was also involved in a terrible accident with that mini bus but he survived only to die few years after of a disease and he was survived by his sister, his wife and two children a girl and a boy.

Frank's niece was a woman who loved God a woman of prayer. Frank had trained her not to follow all those ancestral sacrifices and put her trust only to God. She knew that Jesus has done the sacrifice for those who believe in Him and there were no more sacrifices which were still necessary.

CHAPTER 11

Going back to Frank's concerns of ancestral ceremonies, there were always tombstones unveiling ceremonies in the black communities. This was done after a tombstone had been erected on the grave of the deceased family member. Many believed the deceased person's soul was in that grave and he or she could hear and see them. It was always suggested that the family should visit the grave and talk to the deceased whenever they needed blessings.

To justify the practice of the ceremonies there were Scriptures which pastors liked to quote. The first one was (Genesis 28:12-19) New King James Version whereby Jacob was sleeping at a certain place and had a dream seeing a ladder which was set up on earth and its top reached to heaven. The angels of God were ascended and descended on it.

The Lord stood above the ladder and said: "I am the Lord God of Abraham your father and the God of Isaac; the land on which you lie I will give to you and your descendants. Also your descendants shall be as the dust of the earth; you shall spread abroad to the west and the east, to the north and the south and in you and in your seed all the families of the earth shall be blessed."

"Behold, I am with you and will keep you go and will bring you back to this land; for I will not leave you until I have done what I have spoken to you." When Jacob woke up he said, surely the Lord is in this place and he did not know.

He was afraid and said, "How awesome is this place! This is none other than the house of the Lord and this is the gate of heaven!" When he rose early in the morning he took the stone that he had put at his head set it up as a pillar and poured oil on top of it.

Jacob had put this stone in honour of the Lord because he had an encounter with the Lord in that place. It was distressing to hear the pastors now were distorting this whole Scripture and compare a tombstone unveiling with what Jacob encountered with the Lord because these were completely different scenarios.

Another Scripture which they liked was (Joshua 4:2-7) New King James Version whereby the Lord instructed Joshua to take twelve men from the people, one man from every tribe. That he command them to take for themselves twelve stones from there, out of the midst of the Jordan, from the place where the priests' feet stood firm. That they carry those stones over with them and leave them in the lodging place where they lodged that night.

Then Joshua called the twelve men whom he had appointed from the children of Israel one man from every tribe. Joshua instructed them to cross over before the ark of the Lord their God into the midst of the Jordan and each one of them to take up a stone on their shoulder.

According to the number of the tribes of the children of Israel, that it may be a sign among them when their children ask in time to come, saying". What do these stones mean to you?"

"Then you shall answer them that the waters of the Jordan were cut off before the ark of the covenant of the Lord; when it crossed over the Jordan, the waters of the Jordan were cut off. These stones shall be for a memorial to the children of Israel forever."

This was also a completely different aspect of the commemoration which was the crossing over of the children of Israel from the river Jordan. Where the Lord through His miracles the water of the river was cut off to enable the Israelites to cross. There was no dead person who was left or buried there before they cross to be remembered.

This incident therefore had nothing to do with the celebration of the unveiling of the tombstones of the deceased. There was a certain pastor who had once made a good example of a tombstone. He quoted Genesis 35:20 whereby after Rachel died, Jacob set a pillar on her grave which is the pillar of Rachel's grave to this day.

This pastor related this story so well just to let people know the reason behind of setting up a tombstone so that the relatives should know where they buried their deceased relative.

More than anything it would be nice if all human beings be respected irrespective of their nationality, colour or creed. Or whether are poor or rich and the protection of women and children as they are valued by God. Also most important the salvation of souls up to the ends of the earth as Jesus declared.

There had been an increase of murder of women and children in the most gruesome manner in South Africa. Those who were responsible for committing those crimes were normally compared with animals but this was not a fair comparison, animals did not kill of their kind in this manner.

Babies from one month old had become the victims of rape. In some cases they would not be killed like was done after the rape has been committed. It could be that their lives were spared because they would not be able to identify their attackers as they were still very young to recognise them.

However, what was sad they were left paralysed and declared worthless of ever living a normal life many even infected with HIV/AIDS because their attackers were careers of this disease. People were living in a sick society which had no feelings for human kind which was driven by evil.

The law as well was ever failing the victims because it was either those who committed those crimes were not caught or if they were caught justice would not prevail. In most cases it would be alleged that there was not much evidence to get conviction of the suspects.

In other cases they would be arrested and be convicted but with lighter sentences imposed on them. Although in most cases whether a convict got higher sentence or low was immaterial because they would be released on parole after not even have served the half of their sentences.

Those paroled prisoners did not waste time after they were released they would commit the same or worse crimes than those they were convicted for. You would wonder what has gone wrong you would hear people say there was no more humanity amongst the people of this era as it used to be at some period of time.

The country had not yet overcome recession many people were unemployed. The government on the other hand would be making cheap talks of promising the creation of employment and yet nothing was happening. One would have thought that the recession would not have such a great impact in South Africa.

Just before recession started in South Africa there were times when Frank used to wake up early in the mornings. There was a song he would wake up singing which they used to sing as children when he was still singing in the choir. He did not understand how and why he still remembered this song.

This song was talking about life in general that in the world there is happiness, enjoyment and laugher but when that happiness, enjoyment and laugher were gone. It was tears and agony which were caused by suffering. Frank could not understand what caused him to sing this song in the early hours of the mornings. It was a beautiful song with great melody.

However, it caused some concerns to Frank because he thought there was some trouble which he was soon going to be faced with as this song towards the end was talking about agony and suffering. Also the fact that this song from nowhere after some decades, it came back to his memory it worried him. Only after few months when the whole world was in recession the meaning of this song made sense to him that the Lord through this song was warning him of the recession which was going to take place in the whole world.

Food prices went up almost monthly and were still going up. The government service charges every year were increasing by huge percentage mostly not less than 10%. Yet those service charges you pay were poor or not delivered.

Moreover, residence would receive statements with incorrect charges with huge amounts of money being charged. When trying to rectify that it would be a waste of time because 90% were never rectified. Charity places closed down because of the incorrect charges as they could not afford to pay especially electricity bills.

There had been no intervention from the seniors of the government to take corrective measures. The country had been like it had no leadership. Instead the richest people you find in the country were the government leaders. Black people were afraid to vote ANC out because their fear was if a white government could take over again they might bring back apartheid.

South Africa was a democratic country but unfortunately practically it was in contras. The poor were getting poorer and the rich were getting richer. White farmers were attacked and killed by criminals who were taking advantage of the situation. What was sad, often those farmers who were killed were those who have been trying to help the poor families.

The rate of housebreaking had been high. The residence had not been safe in their own houses because burglaries were taking place during the day or in the evening. It did not make any difference to the criminals they attacked any one whom they felt to target.

It was very sad also to mention that in most work places black people were still despised. Very few got opportunities to occupy high positions. One incident a previous company Frank worked for after it merged with another company. The staff attended some briefing in groups about the merge. All executives were white and there was huge excitement in them.

One of their colleagues asked a question he wanted to know whether the company's intention was to turn the whole company lily white. There was immediate tension and silence from the executive and that employee who asked that question never lasted long with the company they made it sure that they make him feel uncomfortable and resigns.

In Frank's last employment he received a call from one of the employment agents. She was looking for recruits who had experience of the area of his department but she said those recruits needed they should be coloureds or Indians. Frank was very shocked with that kind of a request but on deeper thinking he concluded that he could not blame the agent because what she was requesting was the requirement from her client.

Black people have suffered and died for the struggle unfortunately nothing much had changed for their struggle except the government. South African government had been naïve when it comes to sort problems facing the country but they had been very alive in taking care of their own affairs which affect them personally.

The possible thing which next was going to happen in the country was a civil war something which everybody thought had been overcome. It was imminent and real if true change could not take place. The country had already seen the burning of government buildings and the destruction of properties by the communities crying for better services and other issues related to non-delivery by the government.

Only a miracle could bring a better change, only a divine intervention could come up with true change. Only if the churches could pray, to the only true living God for the bleeding country. It was only the churches which were supposed to have sensed long ago that the country was heading to an iceberg.

The purpose of the church was to stand in the gap for the community to consistently pray for the people that the evil be defeated from all angles. There were many wrongs which the South African government was doing in passing the laws. If churches had come together and pray against those irregularities instead of signing petitions something better could have happened.

The churches should not have compromised the Word of the God. What is good about the prayer you needed not to confront anybody or offend others about what you perceive is wrong. You pray to the Lord and state your case and plead for His intervention. You tell the Almighty God that you do not have the power to change what is wrong which takes place and with Him nothing is impossible because when you are weak He is strong.

You do not have to fight toe to toe with the giant because that would be committing suicide. The battle is for the Lord He will fight for His people. As Paul says in (Ephesians 6:11-15) put on the whole armour of God, that you may stand against the wiles of the evil.

For we do not wrestle against flesh and blood but against principalities, against powers, against the rulers of the darkness of this age, against spiritual hosts of wickedness in the heavenly places, therefore we need to take up the whole armour of God that we may be able to withstand in the evil day and having done all, to stand.

Evil which was taking place in South Africa confirmed that the battle was not black and white but was spiritual and only could be fought spiritually to bring it to the end. Otherwise it would be fighting a losing battle.

When many of Frank's staff members were imposed with impossible requirements they would normally ask him. What he was doing to defend them in those situations but Frank sometimes was tired of fighting.

The church members as well could have stopped fighting for positions like in the corporate world and heed to their calling they could have made a difference. It was most unfortunate that pastors were expected to be served instead of serving the people.

When the very same people who knew the Scriptures very well decided to take life lightly it became a concern. How those who were still in the dark would be able to receive the light? In (Matthew 5:13-16) New King James Version Jesus says, "You are the salt of the earth; but if the salt loses its flavour; how shall it be seasoned? It is then good for nothing but to be thrown out and trampled underfoot by men."

"You are the light of the world. A city that is set on a hill cannot be hidden. Nor do people light a lamp and put it under a basket, but on a stand and it gives light to all in the house."

People can start to see the direction when the light is put on a lampshade. The country can be illuminated when the light flashes from the lamp posts. The country could be able to see the direction when there is an active light. The people could come out of the darkness and go to the direction of the light.

The darkness cannot overwhelm the light. Unfortunately the world was recruiting from the church instead of the church going to recruit from the world. It happened repeatedly during the times of elections. The politicians went and canvased for votes from the churches. They talked about involvement of the churches in political affairs of the county when it was convenient for them.

One could not blame the politicians when they went to the churches to seek what they needed. It was not their fault that the churches were not doing their job. First and foremost it was a confirmation that the government recognised the churches. They were making it easy for the churches to preach the gospel to them. It was like fish handing themselves over to the fishermen.

Still the churches did not see the need to preach to those politicians and emphasised the need of good governance and convert them. One would be upset when seeing the politicians go to the churches to get votes and yet after the elections those government officials disappeared and not deliver the promises.

The churches had the authority to get explanation from the government when things were going wrong within the government as the church voted for the government. They were also authorised to give advice which was according to the Bible. When Paul was arrested by the Hebrews and accused of sedition in (Acts 26:27-28) New King James he was not afraid to speak the truth and address King Agrippa and tell him about the prophets.

During that period Christianity was taboo but Paul did not have a fear to speak the gospel even King Agrippa admitted to Paul that he almost persuaded him to become a Christian.

Paul's response was he would to God that not only King Agrippa but also all who hear him that day, might become both almost and altogether such as he was except for the chains which bound him. This was a powerful statement from a man who was in chains and as well arrested for the same beliefs.

In a free democratic society in the country which has a freedom of speech and whereby the government officials visited churches but the churches were afraid to preach to them. They were afraid to tell them about the wrongs they were doing. They rather entertained them and even failed to pray for those politicians.

The church had failed the nation more than those corrupt politicians as they had the power of prayer and prophecy to change. It appeared like "The great Commission" had no meaning in South African churches. That explained why South African black churches were not involved in missionary.

CHAPTER 12

In some churches new converts who had been promised to be taken care of after the alter call were being neglected and ended up being Christian orphans. Everybody was too busy to remember them and walk with them in their new path.

Salvation of the lost souls was taking a slow pace. During the time of Noah people regarded him as a crazy old man. The churches were supposed to work hard so that the same experience should not take place again.

Christians needed to understand that they had a task upon them to help to bring as many souls as possible to salvation. There was supposed to be seriousness about this task and not look down upon certain class of people. That could help to achieve what the Bible teaches.

The zeal was needed to bring as many souls as possible to salvation and walk with them in growing spiritually. Otherwise the goalpost had been missed. The concentration should not only be on celebrities.

(Luke 4:18) New King James Version; explains that Jesus came to preach the gospel to the poor. He came to heal the broken-hearted. Jesus came to proclaim liberty to the captives and recovery of sight to the blind, to set at liberty those who are oppressed and to proclaim the acceptable year of the Lord.

(Isaiah 61:1) New King James Version also confirms the purpose of Jesus coming to earth as it states that, "The Spirit of the Lord God is upon Me because the Lord has anointed Me to preach good tidings to the poor; He has sent Me to heal the broken-hearted, to proclaim liberty to the captives and the opening of the prison to those who are bound and to proclaim the acceptable year of the Lord.

The teachings of the Scriptures needed to be followed to do the will of God. It was an important task to obey the Lord so that everything should go according to His promises. The situation would become very easy than it looked when the Christians stood in the gap for the nation.

People who went to churches seeking help needed to be taken care of and not to be undermined. They approached churches because of different problems they encountered in life. Those people were coming to cry to the Lord not to inconvenient anybody. They entered the church because they saw the house of the Lord.

The Christians duty was to accept them that they could meet their expectations and the Lord heal and deliver those who were wounded physically and spiritually through the hands of Christians.

The apostles from the first church and the pastors after them were faced with all kinds of persecutions until they were brutally killed. It was very tough it would not be easy for Christians of today to withstand what they went through. It was not a position to be a pastor during the olden days.

The difference could be seen in Paul's situation, in (1Timothy 3:1) New King James Version Paul says, it is a faithful saying that if a man desires the position of a bishop, he desires a good work. The respect and prestige given to Christian leaders of today was not happening in Paul's time. In his time, a bishop was faced with great danger and worrisome responsibility. Rewards for the work of leadership in the church were hardship, contempt, rejection and even death. The leader was first to draw fire in persecution first in line to suffer.

In this light of Paul's explanation he did not encourage misuse by people merely seeking status in the church. Imposters would have little heart for such difficult assignments. To work under dangerous circumstances that prevail in the first century, even brave and determined Christians needed encouragement and incentives to lead. That is why Paul called leadership "honourable ambition."

Leaders of the church in China suffered most at the hands of communists. In many troubled areas today, spiritual leadership was no task for those who seek stable benefits and upscale working conditions. In Paul's day, only a deep love for Christ and genuine concern for the church could motivate people to lead.

In today's church leadership carried prestige and privilege, people aspired to leadership for reasons quite unworthy and self-seeking. High achievement is not a problem but unworthy motivation is wrong.

Real leaders were very few and more often people and groups were looking for real leaders. In the churches there was always a question asked "who will lead?" Throughout the Bible, the Lord was also looking for true leaders.

In (1Samuel 13:14) New King James Version Samuel tells Saul that his kingdom shall not continue. The Lord has sought for Himself a man after His own heart and the Lord has commanded him to be a commander over His people because Saul had not kept what the Lord had commanded him.

In (Jeremiah 5:1) New King James the Lord says to Jeremiah, "Run to and fro through the streets of Jerusalem; see now and know and seek in her open places if you can find a man. If there is anyone who executes judgement; who seeks truth and I will pardon her."

Frank had been deeply moved in seeing people coming into a church looking for salvation if nobody knew them no one cared to make them feel welcome unless they were celebrities or rich well-known individuals.

In (Ezekiel 22:30) New King James the Lord says to Ezekiel, "So I sought for a man among them who would make a wall and stand in the gap before Me on behalf of the land, that I should not destroy it but I found no one."

This is the indication from the Bible that there were not much leaders out there who were committed to full discipleship and prepared to take on responsibility for others and when that person was found was used to his full potential. Those few such leaders who were found they still had shortcomings and flaws and despite those limitations, God accepted them as spiritual leaders.

To be a leader in the church required strength and faith beyond merely average. The need for true leaders in South Africa was so great and candidates for leadership were few. Unfortunately generation after generation the demand for spiritual leadership has been in demand and in most cases could not be found.

In (1Corintians 1:13) New King James Version Paul is questioning the Corinthians as they decided to call themselves the followers of certain leaders, whether Paul was crucified for them, or whether they were baptised in the name of Paul. It was distressful to see some of the church leaders promoting themselves to be followed in South Africa. They went as far as allowing T-shirts to be printed with their face images and the head cloth covering of women having their face images.

One would be rejoicing to see such huge number of people having accepted the gospel but if they were made to believe in following an individual it was disappointing. In (Isaiah 42:8) New King James the Lord says clearly, "I Am the Lord, that is My name and My glory I will not give to another, nor My praise to carved images."

It was very wrong then that this was ignored by the leaders of churches and chose to steal the glory of God. It was wondering whether they became so used to the Lord and the power He allowed them to heal the people that they thought it was of their own power.

Elders in some churches would act in contras from what the senior pastor was teaching. They would not act as Christian elders of the church and have the reservation of whom they wanted to accept as a visitor.

Frank's journey of becoming a Christian as he was visiting some of Christian black churches in some extreme cases he experienced. The duty of the ushers in the church would direct people where to sit as they come into the church. Unfortunately most new converts or visitors would not like to be seated in front. Some would ignore the instructions and sit where they felt comfortable.

There was one incident which Frank experienced, it got out of hand whereby this person had an argument with an usher and did not sit where he was directed. The usher reported the incident to the elders. Instead the issue could be addressed with this particular individual. One of the junior pastors was advised to address the situation with the whole congregation.

After the church had started he addressed the whole congregation that if people would not want to take instructions they should not come to church. He said they should stay at home and not attend the church because they were not welcome. This statement was extraordinary and disturbing because as a Christian you cannot address people in that manner. As there were people who were still new in the church who thought the church was a holy place and full of love.

If they hear this kind of harsh words they would never come back to the church and they would mistrust all the churches and think that it was the normal behaviour of pastors in the church.

There was also another incident whereby an elder who was requested to give a preaching about the offering. Instead of giving a background about the aspect of offering she was attacking people of their behaviour that they were sinners who commit adultery. That the previous night they committed adultery and they were now acting holy and they were playing church.

She went on and criticised the sick who ever went in front for prayers to seek healing. She said they were ever requiring prayers. That was completely out of context and not Scriptural.

The Bible says God is love in (1John 4:8) states that, he who does not love does not know God, for God is love. Frank was bewildered where this hatred comes from in the house of the Lord. This was really crazy act at its worst.

One would believe leaders in the church would not feel threaten of losing their positions to others instead they would have a motive of grooming others for the purpose of serving God and that their purposes in life be fulfilled. They should have the desire to develop other leaders who will take over them when they are not there.

The leaders were supposed to imitate those in the Bible who were worthy of the name leader. The church was in need of committed leaders who were disciplined like the then leaders who lead the way by demonstrating through their lives a faith worth imitating.

They were supposed to study the Bible to be able to know the lives of the former leaders and imitate their faith. One could do introspection and compare their leadership with the leadership of former leaders and make sure the lessons learned from biblical and spiritual leaders they applied in their leadership.

From the ancient time in the Bible Moses mentored Joshua, Elijah mentored Elisha and Paul mentored Timothy. The chain goes on, present leaders needed to keep on cultivating Christian leaders and not to regard new comers in the church as rivals. They should have rejoiced when the house of the Lord was growing.

Like Jesus, in (Luke 5) says that, He found His future leaders fishing at Gennesaret Lake He picked them up just as they were He called them and name them. He named Simon, "Peter." Leaders therefore, needed to know what the names of those they want to develop stand for. They were to know them well understand their strength and weakness and call them by the new vision of what they will become in Christ.

Jesus made a team of His disciples they also knew that in fishing without teamwork they could go broke. Jesus believed in teams, He sent His disciples out by twos. Leadership development needed to know the power of teams. It was important to work with individuals but also to bring them into a group. Where strengths and weakness could be balanced and vision shared.

Jesus's leaders were grown men when He called them and not little kids. Adults become best at their learning when they can be a part of what is already taking place. Jesus's leadership program was not like school, it was life. The disciples were apprentices to Jesus. This teaches the lesson leaders learn in real life situations.

Jesus told His disciples to follow Him at the very beginning He met them. He carried His teachings by letting them to live with Him and watch Him. He then sent them out to go to do, entrusting them with a task. Jesus demonstrated that leaders are made not just by telling them what to do but also trusting them to do the task.

He put them in a test when the great storm came upon them on the lake while He was sleeping on the boat. When they cried to him that they were going to drown. He asked them, "Where is your faith". He pushed them beyond their safe depths. Leaders grow when they are in situations beyond their own control and strength. When they learn that they will fail unless they trust in God.

From the crowd He picked seventy and from the seventy He selected twelve and out of the twelve, He picked three. He frequently took His inner three, Peter, James and John. When He healed the little girl and spoke with Moses and Elijah on the mountain and prayed in the garden He was with the three.

Just to deviate a bit from grooming leaders. Frank's brother in law related a preaching to him by one pastor at the tombstone unveiling. He seemed to have been inspired by this pastor who was telling people that when Jesus met with Moses and Elijah on the mountain. It was a confirmation that the ancestors do exist and they can be contacted therefore black people should continue to contact their ancestors. It was really heart breaking to learn that men of God who were supposed to lead people to the right direction mislead them in that manner.

Instead of the leaders concentrate in their own desires in the church were supposed to have a heart for God as it states in (Matthew 22:37) New King James Version that "You shall love the Lord your God with all your heart, with all your soul and with all your mind." That could help leaders to grow love towards the people.

Love your neighbours and their families as it says in (Matthew 22:39) New King James Version. Leaders should lead and serve like Jesus as in (Mark 10:45) New King James Version says, "For even the Son of Man did not come to be served but to serve and to give His life a ransom for many."

The gospel should be communicated effectively, have passion, thoughtfulness, creativity and integrity like (2 Corinthians 3:5-6) New King James Version says, not that we are sufficient of ourselves to think of anything as being from ourselves but our sufficiency is from God.

Who also made us sufficient as ministers of new covenant, not of the letter but of the Spirit for the letter kills but the

Spirit gives life. Leaders should live humane and holy lives that will make the gospel attractive as it says in (1Timothy 4:12) New King James Version that let no one despise your youth but be an example to the believers in word, in conduct, in love, in spirit, in faith in purity.

Also leaders should be aware of their world and alert to their generation as it states in (Acts 13:36) New King James Version "For David, after he had served his own generation by the will of God, fell asleep, was buried with his fathers and saw corruption." To do the will of God you serve the people of God like David as a leader he served the people until the time arrived that he left this earth.

Jesus also had always talked about serving the people He said the kingdom of God was a community where each member served the others. He defined His ultimate purpose using that term. "For the Son of Man did not come to be served but to serve and to give His life as a ransom for many" (Mark 10:45) New King James Version.

Leaders should act compassionately for the lost and the needy as Jesus did in (Matthew 9:36-38) New King James Version as it says, but when He saw the multitudes, He was moved with compassion for them because they were weary and scattered like sheep having no shepherd. Then He said to His disciples, "The harvest truly is plentiful but the labourers are few. Therefore pray the Lord of the harvest to send out labourers into His harvest."

Leaders needed to be kingdom seekers and not empire builders as (Matthew 6:33) New King James states that, seek first the kingdom of God and His righteousness and all these things shall be added to you.

Leaders should long for the unity of Christ's people as in (John 17:20-23) New King James Version when Jesus was asked by the Pharisees when the kingdom of God would come He answered them and said "The kingdom of God does not come with observation; nor will they say, "See here! Or see there. For indeed the kingdom of God is within you"

Then Jesus told the disciples that the days will come when you will desire to see one of the days of the Son of Man and you will not see it. And they will say to you "Look here! Or look there! Do not go after them or follow them.

Also learn to pray the work as (Matthew 9:35) New King James Version says, and a voice came out of the cloud, saying, "This is My beloved Son hear Him." Leaders needed to maintain a positive environment which is conducive to the growth of people who did not yet possess leadership skills. If they could not keep that environment people would be afraid of growth.

Church leaders needed to keep people they were grooming close to them so that they could begin to learn how they do things. This would have helped people who were not naturally prone toward leadership and had no leadership experience as they often got discouraged easily.

They needed to keep room for mistakes as these people have never been leaders before therefore they were inclined to make mistakes. It was possible that they would make many mistakes in the beginning. It could be also a long process to develop them. When you demonstrate a high belief in them, you encourage them to be determined even when things get rough.

Walk alongside with your trainees as in the beginning they will be reluctant to assume leadership roles and empower them. As you give them authority also affirm them in public to build their confidence. To speedy up their developments it is important to play in their strength as they have experienced few successes in leadership before.

Leaders should bear in mind in everything they were doing that they were in the last days and the last days were characterised by falsehood as (2Timothy 3:1-5) New King James Version states that, the wrong practices are linked with wrong doctrine. When you start to segregate from God's people who arrive in your churches those were wrong practices which are followed by wrong doctrines.

All these are the consequences of men being lovers of themselves, lovers of money, boasters, pride, blasphemers, unholy, unloving despisers of good and lovers of pleasure rather than lovers of God. Most unfortunately when you do these things you might have full churches but all these will be religion without power.

How great it could be as a leader that you preach the Word, be ready in season and out of season. Convince, rebuke, exhort with all longsuffering and teaching and fulfil your ministry.

With Paul it was so beautiful because he practised all his preaching up to the end, in (2Timothy 4:6-8) New King James Version when he was aware that anytime he was going to be killed, he says "For I am already being poured out as a drink offering and the time of my departure is at hand."

With honesty he says, "I have fought the good fight, I have finished the race, I have kept the faith." These are the good words of a man who was faithful to the end and was not swayed by the unworthy things of this world.

In conclusion believe in the Bible and that it was inspired by God and written by human beings and it is without error. Believe in one God, the living and true God, existing in three Persons: - the Father, the Son and the Holy Spirit.

Believe that Jesus Christ is eternal Son of God, became man without ceasing to be God and continues to be the God-Man forever. Believe His death on the cross was a substitutionary sacrifice for the sins of all men and that His bodily resurrection from the dead guaranteed redemption and salvation to all those who believe. Also believe that He later ascended into heaven exalted at the right hand of God where He is our High Priest and Advocate.

Therefore believe that all those who died they will resurrect and those who died in Christ will live eternally and have hope that all your love ones who died in Christ you will meet them on the other side.

End.

Bibliography

Grudem W. 1994. Systematic Theology, Grand Rapids: Zondervan.

Smith KG 2006. The way of love. Crossroads. Johannesburg: South African Theological Seminary

Leighton F 1991. Transforming leadership (Downers Grove, III: Inter Varsity Press).

About the Writer

Thami Nodwele was born in Pretoria South Africa and was raised by his grandmother.

He has a Bachelor degree in Theology. His second book he wrote after "I will meet you on the other side" is "Deliberately Compromised." It tells the captivating tale of an African youth's struggles against oppression set in apartheid South Africa.

Printed in the United States
By Bookmasters